Transracial Adoption: A Follow-Up

Transracial Adoption: A Follow-Up

Rita J. Simon
University of Illinois
Howard Altstein
University of Maryland

LexingtonBooks
D.C. Heath and Company
Lexington, Massachusetts
Toronto

Library of Congress Cataloging in Publication Data

Simon, Rita James
    Transracial adoption, a follow-up.

    Includes index.
    1. Interracial adoption—United States—Longitudinal studies. 2. Children,
Adopted—United States—Family relationships—Longitudinal studies.
3. Intercountry adoption—United States—Longitudinal studies. 4. Race
awareness in children—Longitudinal studies. I. Altstein, Howard.
II. Title.
HV875.S562   362.7′34   80-8770
ISBN 0-669-04357-5   AACR2

Published simultaneously in Canada

Printed in the United States of America

International Standard Book Number: 0-669-04357-5

Library of Congress Catalog Card Number: 80-8770

For
Julian and David, Judith and Daniel;
and for Helene, Sammy, and Rachel

Contents

List of Tables

Acknowledgments

We acknowledge with gratitude the support of the Edna McConnell Clark Foundation who provided funds to carry out and analyze the parents' survey.

We would like to pay our second debt of gratitude to the parents who participated as respondents in our study. Just as they did the first time we contacted them in 1972, so did they on this occasion cooperate with us by giving generously of their time and thoughts. We very much appreciate their helpfulness and cooperation.

Ms. Sally Clemons and the Families Adopting Children Everywhere (FACE) organization provided us with an additional list of parents who participated in our survey for the first time.

Joli Jensen and Mark Fackler helped us code and analyze the data, Laurie McCarthy edited the final draft of the manuscript, and Anita Specht and Marvene Blackmore typed many versions. We acknowledge all of their help with gratitude and appreciation.

1 Introduction

Seven years ago we surveyed parents and children in families who had recently adopted transracially. This book describes what has happened to those families in the intervening years. It focuses on the parents' relations with their transracially adopted child(ren), on the siblings' relations with each other, on the parents' perception of the adopted child's racial identity, and on the parents' expectations about the child's future identity. In the most general sense, it describes how things have been going for each family as a whole: whether the transracial adoption has introduced special strains or problems or provided them with gratifications.

Transracial Adoption, published in 1977, reported the results of our initial contacts with 204 families living in five different cities in the Midwest, each of which had adopted at least one nonwhite child. Most of the adopted children are American blacks; the second largest group is American Indians. There are also a few Korean, Eskimo, and Mexican children. The major purpose of the study was to explore the racial identity, awareness, and attitudes of the adopted and nonadopted children in the families. In addition to the parents in each of the families, we also interviewed some 388 children between the ages of three and eight years.

The children's responses to various projective tests using dolls, pictures, and puzzles constituted the most important finding to emerge from the study. As a group, the children were more racially color blind and more indifferent to race as a basis for evaluation than any other group reported in any previous study, including studies not only on children in the United States but in Hawaii, New Zealand, and other parts of the world. We found black children who did not think that white children were smarter, cleaner, or more attractive than themselves. We found white children who did not think that black children were dumber, meaner, less attractive, and so on. In other words, our results demonstrated that black and white children responded in similar fashion to traditional questions about which doll or which child they would like to play with, or have as a friend, or looks bad.

We also talked to each of the parents in those 204 families. We found that most of the fathers and mothers believed that race did not figure greatly in how people perceived and evaluated each other or the way they would be likely to relate to each other. We found that on the whole, the parents were extremely optimistic about what relations between different racial groups in the United States would be like in the next one or two decades.

They did not seem to be hiding their heads in the sand, disavowing that they, as white parents, would have problems rearing their black or Indian children. On the whole, they believed that their problems would not be insurmountable and that their children would grow up to be emotionally healthy, well-adjusted individuals, able to relate to the culture and society of their adopted parents and to the society of their ethnic origins.

The findings reported in this volume represent a second but not final stage. We plan to talk with both the parents and the children again when most of the children reach their junior and senior years in high school. For this second stage, we decided not to interview the children.

Two hundred and four families comprised the sample for our first study. We were successful in locating 71 percent of the original cases. The remaining 29 percent of the families were unreachable through any of the channels we tried. We contacted local Open Door Societies and COAC (Council on Adoptable Children) officers and consulted membership lists of various other transracial adoption organizations. We asked for information from people who had helped us seven years before. All our leads in these cases resulted in returned "undeliverable" envelopes. While it is unfortunate that we were unable to locate all the original families, we are gratified that we could reach 71 percent of them seven years later.

One hundred forty-three families received our questionnaire and a cover letter reminding them that they had participated in our study seven years before. We explained that we were interested in how things had progressed in the intervening period and that we hoped to interview their children three or four years hence. The questionnaire focused on their relations with their adopted child(ren), on the children born to them, on the children's relations with each other, on what they perceived their children's racial identity to be, and on the ties that both the adopted and the nonadopted children had to their larger family units (that is, grandparents, aunts, and uncles), their schools, and their communities.

The first portion of the questionnaire solicited demographic data for a family update. We asked if any more children had been born or adopted into the family and for details about the children's age, sex, race, and health. We also asked if they were in the process of adopting a child, if they had tried to adopt and were unsuccessful. About other changes in the family, we asked, if children had married or left home for other reasons, or if the parents had separated or divorced.

We asked each set of parents about the racial composition of their neighborhoods and their children's schools. One of the striking findings of the earlier study was that almost all the participants lived in all-white neighborhoods.

With the preceding background information, we then said, "Let's talk about the children we met seven years ago." First, we asked the parents to rate how they characterized their present relationship with their adopted children; we asked them to tell us whether they thought that the relationship was basically positive and good; whether there were problems, but all things considered the positive elements outweighed the negative ones; whether the problems were of such a magnitude that the negative elements outweighed the positive characteristics; or, finally whether they thought things were basically negative and bad. We asked parents about the relationship among their adopted children and siblings that had been born into the family; and if the adoption had produced tensions between them and the children born to them?

The next series of questions concerned the children's performances in school and their relations with peers and teachers. We also asked about friendships and dating. If there were problems, did they stem from racial differences? In a special section on racial identity, we asked parents if their adopted child(ren) identified with a specific racial group. Did the child consider himself or herself black, white, Indian, or mixed? What types of activities or rituals did the family practice to enhance the adopted child's knowledge or identification with his or her racial or ethnic background? To what extent did the adopted child(ren) know the history, culture, and life style of the group into which he or she had been born?

Next on the questionnaire was a series of questions that we had asked in the first study: What was the extent and quality of the ties and relationships that the adopted child(ren) had with various members of the parents' families (grandparents, aunts, uncles, cousins, and so on)? Had the adoption resulted in persistent problems and tensions? Had the adoption brought the family closer together, or had it made little or no difference? How were relations with neighbors and friends? Did the parents perceive a change in their own personalities or in their own definitions of self as a result of the adoption? Then we asked what we knew would be a sensitive question: Had the adoption changed the nature of the relationship between the spouses?

The last part of the questionnaire requested that parents think ahead a few years and anticipate the community in which their adopted child was likely to live. Would the child seek out a community in which the racial characteristics matched those into which he or she had been born? Or would the child(ren) be likely to live in the kind of community in which he or she was reared? Most often those communities were white and middle or upper-middle class. We talked about marriage. What did parents anticipate about the racial characteristics of the spouse of their adopted child?

We asked some questions not directly related to *transracial* adoption but on a topic of interest to adoptive parents: Had their adopted children pressed for information about their biological parents? In the last few years, many child-welfare and social-work agencies, as well as the courts, have been rethinking their almost iron-clad policy on sealed records. In recent years information about their biological parents has become more available to adopted children. We wanted to know if these issues have arisen in the families we were studying. If so, what response had the parents made? We concluded with an openended question: We asked the parents to tell us anything we might have overlooked in terms of their children's adjustment and the family's adjustment to each other.

Of the 143 families who received our questionnaire, 133 completed it and returned it by mail or agreed to be interviewed over the phone. Thus 93 percent of the families we were able to locate participated in the study. Among the 10 families who did not, 9 had responded positively to telephone reminders to return their completed questionnaires but declined to do the interview over the phone (we gave this option to respondents who did not return their questionnaires within two or three weeks after we mailed them).[1]

This volume focuses on the parents' experiences and on their perceptions of how relations with their children have developed between 1972 and 1979, and on how they are likely to develop over the next few years. It also contains information on the current debate between the pro- and antitransracial adoption forces. It reviews court actions and legislation in support of or in opposition to transracial adoption. In an assessment of the regulations and practices concerning intercountry adoption, we describe the results of our survey of another group of families on the East Coast who have adopted transracially and transculturally within the past five years. The children in those families come from Vietnam, India, the Philippines, and other parts of the world. Finally, we examine the policies that the United States is likely to adopt, vis-à-vis adoption generally and transracial adoption in particular. Appendix A summarizes some of the main issues in the debate around sealed or open records and reports the parents' views about open records. Appendix B summarizes and comments on the Model Adoption Act.

Our first volume concluded on a tentative note:

As we have emphasized many times, and wish to do again, it is still too early to say how these children (those transracially adopted and their nonadopted siblings) will develop, whether their "color blindness" and their lack of prejudice or bias toward nonwhites will remain with them as a permanent characteristic or whether the realities of American society will cause alterations in these attitudes. It is also too early to say with whom these adopted children who belong to minority racial and ethnic groups will identify: how they will characterize themselves, with which community their ties will be closest, and how they will relate to their white parents and siblings. If the fears expressed by black and Indian opponents of transracial adoption are realized, that these children will be white on the inside and black on the outside, and that they will be perceived by both white and black as pariahs, transracial adoption will be remembered as a dismal and emotionally costly experiment. If the hopes and expectations of the parents involved in transracial adoption are realized, and their children are emotionally whole, well-adjusted, and able to move easily within the black and white communities, society's failure to maintain and support the program will be remembered with deep regret. Time, thus, will determine transracial adoption's final evaluation.

Returning to these families seven years later, we found that the great majority of the parents continue to believe that they have made a wise and wonderful choice in deciding to adopt transracially. Their lives have been enhanced, enriched, and made more joyous by their decisions. And they still believe that the future for their adopted children and for their families will be a bright one. But for some parents, less than a quarter of them, the problems have been greater than they had anticipated, and bitterness and disillusionment have become everyday emotions. But seven years cannot tell the whole story. The oldest of the adopted children are no more than fourteen. Their own and their families' lives and fortunes may still take many twists and turns. We hope to be able to meet them again four or five years hence to find out from the children directly how they evaluate their life situations. In the meantime we provide a second installment.

Note

1. A brief description of the 10 families who did not participate in the second wave appears in chapter 3.

Part I
The Family Profiles

2 Family Profile

This chapter will acquaint our readers with the demographic and social-psychological characteristics of the families that adopted transracially. In our earlier volume, we discussed the socioeconomic, demographic, and background characteristics of the mothers and fathers in considerable detail.[1] We will review those characteristics and describe changes in the family compositions as a result of separation, divorce, death, additional children (via birth or adoption), and children leaving home to go to school or get married.

Demographic Changes

We noted in the first volume that the families were relatively homogeneous as far as their socioeconomic characteristics were concerned. Sixty-two percent of the mothers had completed four years of college, and 28 percent of them continued on to graduate school. Sixty-one percent of the fathers had university education beyond the bachelor's degree. Sixty-eight percent of the fathers worked as professionals. Most of them were ministers, social workers, or academics. In 1972 none of the mothers held a full-time job outside the home. Almost all of them explained that their decision to adopt had involved a commitment on the wife's part to remain at home as a full-time mother. Forty-six percent of the women had held jobs of a professional nature before they were married or before they adopted their first child.

Of the mothers that we contacted seven years later, at least a third were working full-time outside their homes. For some of them, it was a matter of necessity, for others it was a matter of choice. Among the women who returned to work by choice, almost all were engaged in professional positions of the type they had left at the time of the adoption. The women who worked by necessity were divorced and had become the heads of their households. Most held white-collar or secretarial jobs. One divorced woman went back to work driving a city bus, then moved into the company's public-relations department. Still, the majority of the women chose to remain at home as full-time housewives and mothers.

In 1972 all the families were intact: there were no separations, divorces, or deaths of any of the spouses. By 1979, two of the fathers had died. In one family, both parents died, and the older siblings were raising the younger ones. In one family, the parents were separated, and in 19 families, the parents were divorced. In three of those nineteen, the father had custody of the children.

Only a minority of the families we contacted in 1972 had considered adopting a nonwhite child intentionally. Most of them said they had wanted a healthy baby. When they found that they could not have a healthy *white* baby, they had sought to adopt a healthy black, Indian, or Korean baby, rather than an older white child or a physically or mentally handicapped white child or baby. They preferred a child of another race to a child whose physical or mental handicaps might cause considerable financial drain or emotional strain. About 40 percent of the families intended or wanted to adopt nonwhite children because of their own involvement in the civil-rights movement and as a reflection of their general sociopolitical views. Eighty-one percent of the families had at least one child born to them before they adopted transracially. In many instances, the adoption agency told them to "come back" after they had borne a child.

Twenty-three families have adopted one more child since 1972, and 12 families had another child born to them.[2] Of the children that have been adopted since 1972, 5 are white, 11 are American black, and the other 7 are Vietnamese refugees. Thirteen are boys and 10 are girls. Eighteen percent of the parents reported that at least one child has left home to attend college or to marry.

Neighborhoods, Schools, and Friends

In 1972, 78 percent of the families lived in all-white neighborhoods. Four percent lived in predominantly black neighborhoods, and the other 18 percent lived in mixed neighborhoods. Among the large majority who lived in all-white neighborhoods, only a few planned to move when their adopted children approached school age. Most of the parents saw no incongruity or problems between their family composition and their choice of neighborhood.

Little has changed in that respect over the years. Seventy-seven percent of the families still live in all-white or predominantly white neighborhoods. The others live in mixed communities. Several families living in white neighborhoods have transferred their church memberships to mixed congregations in other neighborhoods. One mother said, "We did this chiefly to give our adopted daughter greater personal acceptance and support there also."

A few of the families living in mixed neighborhoods moved there because they wanted a better racial mix for their children. One parent in a mixed neighborhood reported that of the eight families on their block, four had adopted transracially. Several parents wrote that they plan to move into a mixed community before their adopted children become teenagers.

On the other hand, one parent said that his family had decided to leave a mixed neighborhood because their children were making such observations as, "All blacks steal," and "Most black kids get into trouble with the police." The mixed neighborhood was less affluent than the one in which they had lived previously. The parents said that, indeed, many children were in trouble with the police, and they were mainly black children.

Grow and Shapiro reported that the families in their survey tended to live in totally or predominantly white neighborhoods in relatively small communities. They also noted that "parents in neighborhoods that are not totally white were almost twice as likely as the families in white neighborhoods to report a high degree of satisfaction with their experience in adopting the study child."[3]

Seventy-one percent of the families reported that their children attended mixed schools, and 6 percent said the schools were mostly black. With one exception, all the children in this latter category lived with their mothers after their parents had divorced. A lower standard of living seemed to be represented, as opposed to a different ideological position or commitment.

Based on the racial compositions of the children's neighborhoods and schools, 63 percent of the respondents reported that most of their children's friends were white. Slightly more than a third said their children had both black and white friends, and 3 percent said they had mostly black friends. In the Grow and Shapiro study, about 90 percent of the children had close friends. More than half of these had only white friends. Eight percent of the parents in that study said that their children's best friends were black.

The large majority of our parents characterized their adopted child's school performance as satisfactory. The specific questions we asked were:

How is your adopted child(ren) doing in school?

What sort of student is he or she, and how does he or she get along with his or her teachers?

Seventy-four percent of the parents responded that their adopted children were doing well in school and that there were no academic problems or difficulties with teachers. Fourteen percent said their children were "slow learners" or had some learning-disability problems. Ten percent of the parents said their children were not motivated and were easily distracted. Two percent complained of problems with teachers.

Describing his nine-year-old black son, a father wrote,

> X has never recovered from peer influence in the elementary (and at that
> time a predominant black) school where it was "cool man, not to know."
> He was far behind in reading, writing and mathematics. He is slowly pro-
> gressing with the reading, is below average in sentence structure and spell-
> ing, and will probably fail his math. He has the ability, but it is a game of
> catch up and he is not a worrier, content instead to ride things out. He is,
> however, an excellent musician and a very good athlete.

Describing their adopted black son, a mother wrote,

> T's teachers adore him. He is smart, friendly, considerate, and kind
> hearted. However, at times his behavior is so wild as to drive all the
> teachers and administrators to distraction.

Of her nine-year-old black daughter, a mother wrote,

> She gets along well with teachers and friends. She is a leader, very popular,
> president of her school. She has a glowing personality but is only an
> average student. She had a hard time in 1st grade.

In describing problems, a mother wrote of her two black adopted sons,

> R, in 5th grade is having the first good year in school since preschool. He has
> been the victim of prejudice in school; lack of expectations. His teachers
> wrote him off. Now he is an average student. Our younger son (nine years
> old, also adopted) has a severe learning disability. His school has two
> teachers for seven students. He is having his best year he has ever had.

Another of our questions was, "Has your adopted child had problems
making friends, belonging to peer groups, dating, and other peer-type relations?" Eighty-five percent of the parents said their adopted children have
had no difficulty making friends and belonging to groups. Most of the
parents said their adopted children had not yet started to date.

Over 90 percent of the parents said that their biological children had experienced no problems with peers because he/she had a nonwhite sibling.
One parent, the father of five biological and two adopted children, explained at some length:

> Our children have all been superb in handling any comments that might
> arise. I suspect that few problems have arisen, since we never heard about
> them at home. There is one qualification, when the children first entered
> the public school system here—they attended a predominantly black school
> and so they soon learned how to survive in that scene. The need to protect
> each other simply brought them closer together and the pressures were due

partly to the fact that they were white and partly to the fact that they were bi-racial and living with a white family. Apparently they learned street survival methods well and benefited from the experience.

The mother in the same family wrote,

In a community like ours, our children were probably helped. It was the ''in thing'' to do here.

A father observed:

Our daughter has more problems with her biological brother's long hair than with her non-white brother.

Racial Identity

In 1972 we reported that 65 percent of the families had adopted American black children as their first child (44 percent said the child was of mixed black and white parentage); 11 percent had adopted American Indians; 5 percent, Koreans; 5 percent, Mexicans or Puerto Ricans; and 14 percent, whites. For the second child, 70 percent adopted American blacks; 3 percent, American Indians; 9 percent, Koreans; 1 percent, Mexicans or Puerto Ricans; and 17 percent, whites.

In the more recent study, the racial distribution of the first and second adopted children was almost identical to the preceding percentages. Of those who responded, 65 percent said that they had adopted American blacks as their first adopted children; 11 percent, American Indians; 5 percent, Koreans; 3 percent, Mexicans or Puerto Ricans; and 16 percent, whites. For the second adopted child, 65 percent reported adopting black children (instead of 70 percent); 3 percent, American Indians; 9 percent, Koreans; and the remainder, whites. These responses strongly suggest that the racial characteristics of the adopted children did not account for the families' having moved or for the 10 families who did not respond.

In 1972 we asked the parents how they thought their adopted children identified themselves by racial category. Seven years later the parents were asked the same question, as shown in table 2-1. Note first that all but 3 percent of the parents were able to answer the question. In 1972, 41 percent could not answer because they did not know or did not believe that their children had acquired racial identities. Second, among the 60 percent who did answer seven years ago, 40 percent thought that their children identified as black. In the second wave, 45 percent thought their children identified themselves as black. Twenty-three percent said their children viewed themselves as both black and white. Comparison of the 1979 and the 1972

Table 2-1
Parents' Perceptions of Their First Adopted Child's Racial Identity

	1972	1979
White	19%	15%
Black	24	45
American Indian	5	7
Korean	3	2
Holds mixed identity	8[a]	23[b]
		5[c]
Child is too young to have acquired a racial identity	30	—
Child is confused but beginning to wonder about the matter	8	—
Do not know	3	3

[a]Includes black and white or Indian and black.
[b]Black and white.
[c]Korean and black.

responses shows that 60 percent more parents feel that their children perceive of themselves as black or partly black seven years later.

One mother described her son's identity as "reluctantly black." She wrote,

> We have urged him to accept that he is black. We have tried to make him proud of his black heritage. He now accepts that he is black, but I think he'd be happy to pass for white.

In another family of three children, the father described his two adopted children's racial identifications. His adopted son is black, aged seven and one-half; his adopted daughter is nine and is part black, part Indian, and mostly white.

> J has some problems feeling secure with the toughest black kids in our neighborhood. He has been reluctant for them to know his parents are white for fear they'll tease him. So far he is learning to hold his own despite his fears. He's been practicing judo to build his self-esteem. He has also expressed twice a desire to be white so that he wouldn't be the only different (one). I know I look good brown, but will I always have to be brown? We (the family) assured him we liked him brown even if he was the only brown one—we wanted him that way. This seemed to help. K (nine years old) finds the subject of race and her racial identity pretty painful. In many ways she would like to be white period. Her skin is white, her hair golden brown and "straight." She can pass for white with many people. There is much ahead for her to work through and choose. In some ways she prefers staying young so she won't have to grow up, and she occasionally talks baby talk.

A similar theme comes through in a family with three sons, one of whom is adopted and black. The family lives in an all-white neighborhood. The father writes of his son's identity,

M is mixed, but doesn't like to be called black. He says he wishes he were white like us or sometimes says we should have another black in the family. . . . I hope he does pursue his heritage if he feels unsettled at all about it when he's older. My only disappointment really is when he says he doesn't want to be black or thinks that that's bad. We've tried to promote "Black is beautiful" *and* white is beautiful, but I know children occasionally do call him names like "nigger" and he must be somewhat hurt by it. He usually calls them a name in return and plays with one of his good friends.

A mother wrote,

I tend to forget that she is black. A couple of years ago her little brother hit her on the foot with a hammer. At the hospital emergency room we had to wait a long time for X-rays. People kept coming up to us an asking if this was the little girl who got her foot hammered. They would look at me in what I thought was a strange way. I finally figured out that they thought *I had hit* her with the hammer. For months it bothered me. I mentioned it to a friend who suggested that the people at the hospital were probably just curious about a white mother with a black child.

A father wrote,

I don't think American society really has a classification of racially mixed, but that is how the boys identify themselves. When we adopted the boys I thought that we as a family would have more identification with black culture than has happened. Our girls (who were born to them) have a greater awareness of racial matters than they otherwise would and that seems positive to us. We think all four children like themselves and regard themselves as persons of worth capable of good relationships, of assuming normal responsibilities, and of being members of a caring family.

The increased percentage of parents who perceive racial awareness in their children and a belief that their adopted children have acquired a racial identity (as black or black and white, as opposed to nothing) represents a major change over the seven-year time span.

In 1972 we asked the parents about their preferences for the racial identity their adopted children might acquire in the future. Twenty-five percent said they had no preference. Twenty-two percent said they hoped their child would acquire the identity that his/her racial characteristics imposed, as well as the racial identity of the family (white). Another 11 percent would not answer the question and said they wanted their adopted child to identify with the human race. Of the remaining 42 percent, 24 percent said they preferred black, 12 percent said white, 5 percent Indian, and 1 percent Asian.

A fairly typical response reported in 1972 is the following.

> It's his decision, not ours. Hopefully, we will raise him with an identity toward both groups because he is both white and Negro, and if he wants to identify with one group, that's his decision. I would hope that as a mulatto child, and since there are many mulatto children, that he might feel a part of a new kind of race, and of having the potential of both races within him, such as exists in Hawaii where the people are all mixed races. I would feel better if he chose to identify with the blacks than if he chose to identify with the whites, because I really feel that if he tries to pass for white, we have not done our job as parents. But if he wants to identify with blacks, this is legitimate because legally he is a Negro child and as far as society now exists in 1972, he is a Negro child. To most whites, he is not a mixed race. So therefore, I can't say what society will be like twenty years from now, but as it is right now, hopefully he will identify with the Negro race simply because that's what he is now. Society views him as Negro.

About their children's future racial identities, 21 percent felt that they could not make any useful prediction in 1972 because their children were too young. Four percent said whatever racial identity the children assumed would be all right with them. Thirty-one percent hoped their children would identify as white, 24 as black, 3 percent as Indian, and 1 percent as Asian. Thirteen percent said black and white, and the other 4 percent offered some other combination such as Indian and black or Korean and black.

Seven years into that future, then, in 1979, 45 percent said that their children identified themselves as black.

After asking about their children's current identity in our 1979 survey, we said to them:

> Think ahead a few years to when your adopted child is an adult. Do you anticipate that he/she will live mostly in the community in which he/she has been reared, or will he/she seek out a community whose racial or ethnic characteristics match his or her background?
>
> Do you anticipate that your adopted child will marry a person whose racial or ethnic characteristics match his or hers?

In response to the first item, 38 percent of the parents felt that adulthood was a long way off and were not prepared to guess about the type of community their adopted children would choose. Among those who did answer, very few expected their children to live in a black community. Slightly more than 50 percent thought their children would live in the same type of community in which they had been reared, that is, white, middle-class neighborhoods. The other 2 percent thought the child would seek out a mixed neighborhood; the type one is likely to find in university communities such as Madison, Wisconsin, or Ann Arbor, Michigan. According to the parents, that was the type of community in which their child was reared, accustomed to, and comfortable with. Their lack of experience in black neighborhoods would make it difficult for them to adjust. Those parents who answered that their children would live in a white community also said that their children were accepted as white or were being reared as a white person. One mother reported that her nine-year-old black son wants to move to the African Plains when he grows up and live self-sufficiently with nature and animals in a treehouse.

Sixty-four percent of the parents would not speculate on their children's future spouse. The third or so of the parents who did venture a response were divided almost evenly among white, mixed, and black. One mother, who had commented that the family did not do much in the way of observing black culture, said, "I hope maybe a black woman might be able to give him the cultural background his parents can't." A father wrote,

> Our children have been raised in a home atmosphere where race has no bearing on relationships. I suspect she [a black nine-year-old daughter] will feel free to seek out someone on the basis of personality, not race; and given the greater freedom of women to do the initiating today, I suspect she will have a relatively easy time of it.

The responses requiring parents to consider their adopted children's future community and marriage indicate that many are not ready to come to grips with these issues. Most of the parents hope that they can delay giving hard thought to these matters until they become pressing. Results show that about 25 percent of the parents expect their adopted children to pass as white. Their children are of mixed background and probably look as white as their nonadopted siblings. For black social workers and others opposed to transracial adoption, these figures will have considerable importance.

In 1972 we inquired about parents' efforts to help their adopted children identify with their own racial group. Eight percent responded that the children were still too young to do anything along those lines. Twenty-six percent said that they were doing very little, either by conviction or convenience. They emphasized that they were putting most of their efforts into living together as a family. Two thirds of the parents described sharing books, music, pictures, crafts, and so on about their children's cultures. They talked about trips they would take, groups or clubs that they have joined and plan to join, and activities they have or will engage in to enlighten their children and give them a sense of appreciation for their racial heritage and background.

One of the families who had adopted an Indian child offered the following:

> We're reading a lot of books. We are also buying books so he will have easy access to them once he gets older. We just got some small pamphlets put

out by the Vermillion Indians in South Dakota which have concepts of Indian culture in them. Probably on the 4-, 5-, 6-year old level. We've had some contact with the Indian community. We talked to a girl who called about COAC stuff, and we said we were interested. We arranged a picnic for Indian families and families that had adopted Indian kids. When the Sioux kids who were going around through the Youth Understanding Exchange were in town, we went over to see their show and talked with them. It's mostly a matter of trying to explain Indians to him and letting him meet other Indians so he can see they are real people. We try to avoid TV shows that have Indians on them, unless there is a very unusual one, and it has an historically correct view. It's hard at his age level. It goes through and gets lost. We went to the Pow Wow last summer, and the ones who were dressed up were fine, but the others he didn't think were Indians. I think we're doing O.K. so far. A year ago I would have said no. But I think it's come this year.

Seven years later the range and types of responses were much the same. About a third of the families are doing little or nothing in the way of acknowledging or teaching the adopted children about their backgrounds. The other two thirds help mainly by exposing their children to books, magazines, music, TV, and movies. Almost every family who had adopted a black child commented that they all watched "Roots" together. Several families said that they attend a church in which all or a majority of the congregation are black. About 10 families have black godparents for their adopted children. One mother said, "I keep up a running verbal history lesson." Others noted that their children's school was doing an excellent job of integrating the curriculum, using a variety of multiracial and multicultural materials. Thirty-five percent of the families claimed that they observe the holidays of the particular groups from which their adopted children came.

One family wrote, "We observe Frederick Douglass's and Martin Luther King's birthdays. We have experimented with Ghanian, Morrocan, Irish, Russian, and American Indian recipes, and we have learned African and American Indian songs and music and a lot about African holidays."

Another family said, "We make a point of attending different ethnic groups' cultural events." One family with two sons born to them and two black adopted daughters spent two years in Liberia, where the father worked as an engineer.

Some families "do nothing" because they lack the time. Most, however, do nothing because they do not approve of treating their adopted children as "special"—at least in the sense of catering to his or her exotic cultural backgrounds. One family said, "We do nothing because we are confused about what to do. We have no black friends." Another family stated their position as follows:

We try to watch TV programs like "Roots," go to movies, and read books about people with African heritage. We're not too great at observing any ethnic holidays in our family so we don't make a big thing about our adopted son's ethnic background either. I feel it would be inconsistent, and if we did for him we'd be obligated to look into Scotch, Cuban, Norwegian, German, Bohemian, Danish and Irish ethnic celebrations too. It would probably be a very good education and would be a good school project, but we have lots of other things to teach and do together with our children.

Almost all the families with adopted Korean children have Korean artifacts in their homes, experiment with Korean cooking, and read books about Korea. A few said they plan to visit Korea as a family when their son or daughter is older. One family is studying language tapes and children's song tapes from the library.

Grandparents, Other Relatives, Friends, and Neighbors

Seven years ago 28 percent of the parents perceived grandparents and aunts and uncles as approving and positive about their decision from the outset. Thirty-five percent reported that most of their close relatives initially assumed a negative and disapproving stance but were coming around to acknowledge their own relationship to the adopted children. Their families, they said, were speaking and generally on friendly terms. Thirty-one percent said that their close relatives rejected the adopted children and were not reconciled with the parents. The other 6 percent reported that contacts had been resumed, but the parents felt that the relatives were nervous and apprehensive in their interactions with the children and with them.[4]

Some parents described comical instances in which the grandparents were initially shocked, hostile, and rejecting, and later came to love and feel attached to their new grandchildren. Their general attitude, however, as expressed in the language they used in reference to blacks or Indians or Asians, did not change at all. They still referred to blacks as "niggers" and to Asians as "gooks" or "chinks." They continued to make derogatory remarks about the laziness, dumbness, untrustworthiness, and so on, of such people. One mother said, "My inlaws are still bigots, but they love the kids."

Some respondents became reconciled with their parents after a period of estrangement that centered around the adoption. They described elaborate arrangements whereby they did not visit their parents at their parents' homes (especially when it was in another city) or, if they did, they did not sleep in their parents' houses.

When we questioned these families seven years later on extended family relations, 12 percent reported that the rift about the adoption continued. In some instances, it had deepened, and the family ties had been broken.

About 10 percent said that only a scar remained from the initial negative reaction because parents and children or siblings had managed to patch things up. One husband said that his wife's parents had disowned her for almost a decade, but that ties were reestablished with them last year: "There is still tension, but it is decreasing." Another respondent said that her family cut her off for three years, but they have now resumed relations. One father reported that two of his sisters do not give Christmas or birthday presents to his children, but they do give presents to their other nieces and nephews. The father commented that this behavior causes some problems because of the closeness of the extended family, "When we get together for holidays and birthdays, we tell our kids that the hostility is directed to us as a family, and not to any individual members."

Fourteen percent of the parents said that the adoption had served to bring them closer to their own parents: "It enriched our relationships with family members. Our parents are as loving to their adopted child as they are to their other grandchildren." One family said,

> The adoption [of two black girls] did not affect our relations with our parents, but we believe it has changed *their* outlook about themselves. My husband's parents visited relatives in Sweden several years ago and found themselves staunchly defending the adoptions which they had originally been against. They now live in Florida and are outspoken in their Lutheran church about racial matters.

The large majority of our respondents reported that the adoption had not resulted in an important change in their relations with parents and other relatives. They also felt that initial hostility and skepticism had long since disappeared.

Grow and Shapiro found that "the more contact the parents had with their relatives, the stronger the expression of satisfaction with the adoption."[5] Our study revealed no relationship between satisfaction about adoption and the extent or quality of family ties.

Only a handful (9 percent) of the 1972 respondents reported any negative changes in their relations with friends because of the adoption. Twenty-seven percent felt that some of their friends had drawn closer to them as a result of the adoption. For a few of the families, their friends served as role models and sources of information about transracial adoption. The others did not notice that the adoption made any change in their choice of friends or in the quality of their relationships.

Seven years later, the response pattern was much the same. The large majority of the respondents felt that there were a few changes as a result of the adoption. Fifteen percent said that they had drawn closer to some friends because of the adoption, and 5 percent said they lost a friend or circle of friends as a result of their transracial adoption. One mother said,

"A close friend of mine told me, 'Your son is a safe person to act out your grand liberalism on. He is so handsome and such a good athlete.' " A few respondents commented that their friendships had become more diversified: "We have developed friends of different races that we would not have searched out."

Neighbors initially played relatively unimportant roles in almost all the families. In 1972, for example, only 6 percent of the respondents reported negative reactions by their neighbors. They usually took the forms of forbidding their children to play with the adopted children or not welcoming the children into their homes. Interestingly, unlike the direction of the ties with relatives and friends (where relations improved over time), more families reported negative reactions and difficulties with neighbors in 1979. In our earlier survey, 21 percent of the respondents felt that the neighbors' reactions were positive and that relationships were good. In 1979 only 6 percent of the respondents made that assessment. In 1972 6 percent of the families reported difficulties and negative reactions, but in 1979 that figure was 13 percent. In the earlier survey, all the adopted children were less than 8 years old, and many were preschoolers. Seven years later, however, some of the children were entering adolescence. They were all bigger, more visible, and perhaps noisier and more assertive. Two families reported receiving hate mail and suggestions that they move.

Personality Changes and Changes in Relationship with Spouse

The parents were asked if the adoption had produced changes in their own personalities or in their definitions of self. Many said changes had indeed occurred, and that those changes were neither trivial nor ephemeral in nature. In 1972, 81 percent had reported that some changes had occurred. Twenty-six percent explained that because their transracially adopted children were their first child, they found it difficult to separate the impact of the adoption from the impact of having become parents for the first time. Others stressed that having a black or an Indian child increased their racial awareness and social consciousness as no other event in their lives had ever done. They felt that they had become more aware of manifestations of prejudice. They believed more strongly than before in the importance of treating people equally and not emphasizing distinctions that stemmed from racial characteristics.

A few parents said the adoption had made them realize how prejudiced they had been and, to some extent, still were. Now that they were parents of a black child, however, they felt they must face up to their prejudice, and, in most instances, do something about it. One family put it this way: "We have to work extra hard to stamp out this residue of racial bigotry in ourselves."

When asked, "What race do you consider your family to be?" Forty-five percent answered mixed or interracial, 22 percent answered human, 3 percent answered no racial category, and the others said white. A mother wrote,

> We consider ourselves a black family. I have become constantly aware of blackness and have taught black history courses at local schools and gave pulpit editorials at church. At the same time, I know where my white friends are coming from. They have moved on to women problems, but I continue to feel black ones.

While the mothers felt this more than the fathers, it was by no means only a mother's or a woman's response.

The following question was, "Did your own racial identity change after the adoption?" Thirty percent answered that it did. In essence, they said that they no longer identified themselves as white; they felt that as parents of black children, they had either internalized the experience of being black or had become part of the black consciousness.

Regarding changes that the adoption might have produced in themselves, 72 percent said that it had affected them in important ways. With seven years' hindsight, not all of them saw the effect in a positive light. Nine percent of the parents noted that the problems they were having with their adopted children made them feel inadequate, giving them a negative feeling about themselves and a sense of failure. A still smaller group was bitter at having undertaken something that wasn't working as well as they had hoped and anticipated.

For the large majority, however, the changes were positive. They felt a sense of fulfillment. They said that the transracial adoption gave their lives new purpose, that it offered challenges they responded to energetically. They felt rewarded by the relationships they had with their adopted children. It made some parents' lives more interesting because it introduced the possibility of greater variety of people and friends. One mother wrote, "I appreciate the larger variety of children brought around by our children. They expand my husband's and my own group of friends as we get to know them and their families."

Another mother wrote, "I was 38 at the time we adopted transracially. That experience changed me from an ordinary housewife to an active civil rights worker and community program developer."

Some parents commented on their changed reactions to racial issues in American society: "I have a more personal investment now in the reality and effects of racism in our culture." Not unexpectedly, only 20 percent of the mothers said that the adoption had no effect on their personalities, while 37 percent of the fathers felt that way. A mother wrote,

The other children [there are four older children, all of whom were born into the family] are able to have good relationships with minorities and are able to accept all people because they share this love for their brother. It is really hard to put into words all the good things I feel. I do realize that as he grows older there will be problems, but at this point I feel there are none that we can't help him work out.

Another wrote,

I have done in life what I wanted to do and what I felt was right. No one else was standing in line to take him. No one was even interested in looking at him.

On another dimension, a mother explained,

I had been sent to a juvenile detention home when my own parents were divorced. I saw in my decision to adopt transracially that I was taking a child no one wanted. I wish that I had been wanted enough to be adopted by some family.

In this instance, the mother regards the transracial adoption as her effort at making right her own abandonment.

A father made this observation,

As a consultant to the city's school system, I lead several hundred field trips a year. I know kids all over town. I get a lot of positive strokings in public. But at home, I can't manage my older son. I have not succeeded in opening him up. It shakes my faith in myself.

Along these same lines, another father wrote,

He shakes my self-confidence. My job draws very positive vibrations from hundreds of teachers and thousands of students. Thus when he unloads on me about not caring or runs away, it is a real blow.

At the end of the questionnaire, another father wrote about his twelve-year-old Indian son,

He is a healthy child. In a one-on-one setting, he and I do very well. I like him as a companion on trips. He is very alert to his surroundings and eager to fill in gaps about how things work, etc. If I were to set up an ideal environment for him, it would include lots of space (a farm), pets, a workshop where he could putter and tinker. Trees and fields and places to be active and/or quiet. He would have a lot less opportunity to watch TV and lot more situations involving teamwork and concern for others.

In the more recent survey, we asked the parents if the adoptions had affected their relations with their spouses. Thirty-nine percent felt no effect.

About 40 percent said that they thought the adoption had brought them closer to each other. They now share goals and commitments to a life style they had not anticipated when they married. A few of the respondents said the closeness resulted from a need to close ranks in the face of a common adversary. One parent expressed it this way:

> We have four kids. If we ever run out of a topic of conversation, we can always discuss our son B; his problems have driven us to despair, but his beauty, intelligence, personality and love are also the light of our lives.

On the other hand, 20 percent of the parents were concerned that the adoptions had caused marital strains. The problems of coping with their adopted children had been more than they had anticipated. The parents often found themselves on opposite sides of an issue affecting their relations with the adopted children.

Forty-five percent of the fathers reported that the adoption had no effect on their relations with their wives. Only 33 percent of the mothers felt the adoption had no effect. The mothers were more inclined to see the adoption as having had positive effects on their relations with their husbands. Forty-one percent of the mothers observed positive effects, as opposed to 33 percent among the fathers.

Grow and Shapiro reported that 33 percent of the mothers and 25 percent of the fathers in their study perceived no change in their marital relationship as a result of the transracial adoptions. Four percent of the mothers and 5 percent of the fathers thought their marriages had suffered. The large majority (63 percent of the mothers and 70 percent of the fathers) said they felt they had happier marriages as a result of the transracial adoptions.[6]

Toward the end of our interviews, we asked the parents if the adopted children wanted to know about their biological parents. If they did want to know, how strong or insistent was their interest? A little more than a third of the parents (37 percent) reported that their adopted children had expressed no interest or curiosity about their biological parents. Forty-seven percent assessed their children's interest as mild, and 16 percent said their children had expressed strong and persistent interest. Almost without exception, the parents claimed they would help their adopted children get as much information about their biological parents as they could. Some said they were strong supporters of open records but wanted to wait until the adopted children were eighteen before they began searching for clues on the parent's whereabouts. (The open-records issue and the parents' responses are discussed in greater detail in appendix A.)

Notes

1. See Rita Simon and Howard Altstein, *Transracial Adoption* (Wiley Interscience, New York, 1977), pp. 47-48, for an overview of the League's position statements on transracial adoption from 1958 to 1973.

2. When these parents were asked in 1972 whether they planned to adopt any more children, 20 percent said they did, 41 percent said they did not, and 39 percent had not made up their minds. In many instances, finances were an important consideration. As it turns out, 18 percent of these families did adopt at least one more child.

3. Lucille J. Grow and Deborah Shapiro, *Black Children—White Parents: A Study of Transracial Adoption* (Child Welfare League of America, New York, 1974), p. 88.

4. Simon and Altstein, *Transracial Adoption,* p. 96.

5. Grow and Shapiro, *Black Children,* p. 165.

6. Ibid., p. 81.

3 Special Families

This chapter profiles three types of families who have special characteristics or problems. The families share many of the same qualities of the composite profile described in the previous chapter but are sufficiently different to warrant separate analysis. The family types we have identified are: those who see themselves as having difficult relationships with their adopted children and who feel that the negative elements outweigh the positive ones in their relationships; families who describe themselves as "blessed," characterizing themselves as "special" in the most positive sense, or feeling they have "a stewardship from God"; and single-parent families, either because of divorce or the death of a spouse.

The last section reviews the 10 families who participated in our 1972 survey but who did not respond to the more recent 1979 questionnaire.[1] We will attempt to gain insight into their refusals by reviewing what we know about them from interviews conducted in 1972. The small number of such families (7 percent) aroused our curiosity: Perhaps they share some unusual characteristics that might have allowed us to predict a lack of response.

We shall be discussing a total of 68 families: 23 single-parent families, 25 problems families, 10 blessed families, and 10 refusals.

Problem Families

In his summary of adoption studies conducted between 1924 and 1968 by 15 different researchers, Kadushin reported that 74 percent of the adoptions could be characterized as "unequivically successful;" 11 percent were "fairly successful," "intermediate," showed "some problems" or were "questionable"; and 15 percent were "unsatisfactory," "unsuccessful," "poor," or "problematic."[2] The studies involved 2,236 families, although none involved transracial adoption. In all the studies, success was measured by the level of satisfaction in the experience expressed by the parents.

A second measure, also relying on the parents' subjective experiences, was their response to the following:

Looking back over the whole experience with (name of child), I feel it has been

_____Extremely satisfying

_____More satisfying than dissatisfying

_____About half and half

_____More dissatisfying than satisfying

_____Extremely dissatisfying

Both measures produced similar distributions—about 73 percent were characterized as successful.

Grow and Shapiro applied comparable criteria to the 100 families in their study who had adopted transracially.[3] Their study was conducted in the early 1970s and focused on black children in white families, of at least six years of age, and on children who had been in their adoptive homes for at least three years. The average age of the children was nine, and they had been in their adoptive homes for an average of seven years. Grow and Shapiro reported that, "Seventy-seven percent were judged to represent successful adoptions."[4]

The findings in this study . . . indicate a level of success approximately the same as those obtained in other studies . . . both for traditional white infant adoptions and non-traditional adoptions involving racial mixture and other children.[5]

Table 3-1, adopted from Grow and Shapiro, compares success rates for different types of adoption.

Our study was not directly concerned with success or the lack of it, but we did assess parental satisfaction by asking our respondents the following.

Now we'd like to ask about the children we met seven years ago. How would you characterize your present relationship with your adopted child(ren)? If more than one child is involved, please answer for each child separately. Would you say it was basically good, happy, positive, etc? Are there more positive or more negative elements in the relationship? Please check the appropriate category on the scale below.

_____Basically positive and good.

_____There are problems, but the positive elements outweigh the negative ones.

_____The problems are such that the negative elements outweigh the positive ones.

_____Basically negative and bad.

Table 3-1
Comparison of Success Rates

	Percent
Summarized rate for 11 studies of white infant adoption[a]	78
Racially mixed[b]	72
Japanese[c]	89
Older white[d]	73-78
American Indian[e]	88

[a]Alfred Kadushin, *Child Welfare Services* (Macmillan, New York, 1972), p. 483.
[b]Esther B. Nordlie and Sheldon C. Reed, "Follow-up on Adoption Counseling for Children of Possible Racial Admixture," *Child Welfare* 41 (7) (September 1962):304.
[c]Marianne Welter, *Comparison of Adopted Older Foreign and American Children*, unpublished doctoral dissertation, Western Reserve University, 1965, p. 126.
[d]Kadushin, *Adopting Older Children*, p. 63.
[e]David Fanshel, *Far from the Reservation: The Transracial Adoption of American Indian Children* (Metuchen, N.J.: Scarecrow Press, 1972) p. 333.

The families included in this section answered the preceding question by checking, "The problems are such that the negative elements outweigh the positive ones," or "Basically negative and bad." Also included in this group are families whose descriptions of their relations with their adopted children indicated that there were serious difficulties stemming either from the adoption, from differences in race, or both. Altogether, 25 sets of parents described problems related to the adoption and/or to the racial difference between themselves and their adopted children. We did not include problems that the parents labeled, "sibling rivalry," "parent-adolescent difficulties," or "school-related matters." Only problems that the parents believed to have arisen as a result of their decision to adopt a child of a different race were included. Since about 19 percent of our families fell into these categories, our results compare well to those reported by Grow and Shapiro and those summarized by Kadushin.

The most common episode related by the problem families shows the adopted child stealing from his parents and siblings, being antagonistic and insulting toward them, and doing poorly in school. Most of these parents reported that siblings have had locks put on their bedroom doors to prevent the problem child from stealing money, clothing, and bikes. When confronted by the parents, the child typically lies, denies that he has taken the missing items, and is abusive toward his parents or siblings. In almost every one of these families, the problem child is a male. His race, ordinal position in the family, or number of siblings does not seem to matter.

Also common among the problem children were physical and/or mental or emotional disabilities. The parents believed these to be either genetic or the result of indifferent or abusive treatment in foster homes. The parents expressed bitterness and resentment toward the adoption agency and the social workers, believing that they withheld information that might have influenced their decision to adopt that particular child.[6]

The third scenario is less common than the first two but worthy of comment. Some parents expressed guilt at having inflicted harm on their biological child(ren) through their decision to adopt transracially. They feared that the biological child(ren) suffered neglect as a result of the time, energy, and attention that the adopted child required due to some emotional or physical scars or handicaps. They also noted that the family changed its life style in order to participate in the adopted child's culture. Examples include families' moving into largely black neighborhoods, joining a black church, trying to build a social life around black friends, and observing and celebrating events in black history.

In their account of the 29 problem families in their survey, Grow and Shapiro stated:

> In 13 of the families in trouble, there was little or no evidence that the child's racial identity was a contributing factor to the problem, which might just as easily have developed in the case of a white adoptee or a biological child. In the other 16, however, there was evidence that problems concerning race were at least part of the total problem and, in some instances, the central problems. In two of these families, the parents had apparently been extremely naive about the racial aspects of the adoption. In both instances, the study child had been placed for foster care in infancy. The foster parents had decided to adopt rather than risk giving up the child, apparently without anticipating the impact the racial difference would have as he grew older. In nine cases, there was evidence that the child was in some conflict about his racial identity and his parents were having difficulty in dealing with it. In the remaining five cases, the parents showed a strong tendency to deny the child's racial background by minimizing its importance or passively ignoring it. This was sometimes justified by the child's fair appearance or by lack of specific information about his background. In a few extreme cases, children with a clearly Negroid appearance had not been told of their adoption or their black biological parentage.[12]

Scenario 1

The first of the three situations characteristic of our problem families is also the most common: The adopted child is lying, stealing, cheating, doing badly in school, and being antagonistic and sullen at home.

Most often, the theft victims are members of the child's family: usually his or her siblings. One parent reported that older black boys bribe their twelve-year-old adopted black son to steal from them (for example, his sister's bicycle, money out of his mother's purse) and from other families who live in his affluent neighborhood. One adopted boy was caught breaking and entering into his coach's house. Another family reported that one of their black adopted sons denied that he had stolen from his siblings or neighbors even when he was caught with the goods in hand.

The parents' commitment in these cases is interesting and reassuring. Almost all of them remain optimistic about their future relations with the child who steals and lies. For example, one mother wrote of her thirteen-year-old adopted Indian son who stole from his eighteen-year-old sister,

> Adoption has made me know that I have a universal love of all children regardless of origin. It has made me stretch to understand and help my own particular child.

At the end of the questionnaire, she continued:

> Our adopted child is loving and enthusiastic toward his family. He is a piece of sunshine most days, but he need lots of guidance from both his parents which "tries us" a lot! He is a dear boy and my determination is to help him find his place in the world.

Another mother of 15 children, 12 of whom were adopted, wrote:

> Our newest son came with problems of lying, stealing, bed-wetting, unable to learn, but he's going to be O.K. We still believe in adoption and thank God for each of our 15 children. Yes, there have been tears and trials, but through them we've all grown and become better people. There's been a lot of joys and triumphs too, and we're proud of this family of ours.

The behavior of an adopted Indian son seems to have greatly disrupted relations in another family. The father describes the boy as "brow-beating the family." He is twelve years old and is seeing a therapist twice a week. He steals clothing and money from his parents and siblings and has threatened his older brother and younger sisters with a kitchen knife. He has attacked his older brother (who is fourteen and born into the family) and his younger brother (who is seven and adopted from Latin America). The older children have locks on their rooms. The father describes the adopted son as "devious, sneaky, and a thief."

The siblings often tell their parents that it was a mistake to have adopted him. Several years ago the boy became involved in exploring and identifying his Indian background, but that interest has waned in the last year or so. The whole family became involved with the Indian School, but the boy's interest has lessened with each year. He generally ignores books about Indian culture that are available at home. The friends he has are white. The school he attends is 80 percent white, 20 percent black. The boy's behavior also has caused problems between the parents, because they "sometimes disagree about how to handle specific incidents with E and criticize each other's reactions. He plays one against the other." The mother wrote, "I feel much less adequate as a parent than I used to."

Both parents, but especially the mother, are more pessimistic about the future than most parents. Concerning who E might marry and where he might live, the moter wrote,

> I have no idea. He's *very* self-centered—more so than our other kids, including the youngest who is also adopted. [It is] hard to see him in a successful marriage unless he learns some giving to go with his usually taking. I don't see him as seeking an Indian community—and he'd have difficulties in one, probably.

Another mother described problems they are having with one of their adopted sons.

> He acts as if he has no conscience. He is totally dishonest. He steals constantly. He gets along with no one. The other children have had to lock their bedroom doors even if they are just going to the bathroom. I'm amazed at how well they get along in spite of his stealing. It's hard to love your 12 year old brother who will steal your new bike and sell it for a dollar and swear he didn't touch it.

> He is very difficult to live with, but race has nothing to do with it. His race has augmented the problems, because as a dishonest person with no morals, blacks bribe him to steal from us and neighbors in our professional neighborhood. He'll do anything for a candy bar. He came to us unable to leave the table as long as any food was left on the table and has been food crazy his whole life.

> I keep hoping and expecting he'll eventually grow out of this, given enough love and permanency. He reads a grade above his level. I have worked hard on supplying him with good books, hoping his ability will get him through. He's also a good athlete and we've gotten him into ice hockey leagues etc. to help him feel capable and a member of teams, boy scouts, too. He has really presented a challenge.

Scenario 2

The family whose child has PKU[8] is the most dramatic example of parents who feel bitter and betrayed by the adoption agency and their social worker. C is now fourteen years old. Since February 1977, she has been in a state hospital. She comes home on weekends and for short vacations.

C's parents had had one child born to them two years prior to the adoption. After adopting C, the mother gave birth to two more daughters. They had tried to adopt before their first child was born. Their only adoption requirement was that the child be healthy: age, sex, and race were relatively unimportant. The adoption agency put them off by urging them to wait to adopt until they had been married longer, and, if possible, until they could bear a child. The couple returned after their first child was born and indicated that they still wished to adopt a child. By this time they were quite sure they wanted a nonwhite child. A two-year-old American Indian girl was available. The parents were delighted, and the child was placed in their home. At the time of the adoption, the parents were unaware that C was suffering from phenylketonuria (PKU). It is not clear from their story whether or not the social worker knew.

During our first interview with the parents in 1972, the mother related their early discussions with the social worker. They did not think they could cope with a child with emotional problems or with one who was dull or hard to teach or had difficulty learning. That was the one condition they had placed on the adoption agency. The mother now feels, "We got exactly what we didn't want. We don't suffer the guilt problems, necessarily, but we are feeling very sad about the whole business, and finding it hard to be in public."

Five years passed between our initial contact with the family and the time they decided to commit C. Relations between C and her parents and between C and her siblings deteriorated drastically. Her temper tantrums and her anger got worse. She stole money from her younger sisters. The other children were shunned by the neighborhood because of C's bizarre and aggressive behavior. The mother wrote,

> C is not very cooperative and our personalities do not work well together. We antagonize each other. She is very emotionally immature, and she still provokes people. She hangs on to me, but hates me and her own dependence. Everything we ask her to do is a war. She doesn't want to please any one at all.

> C steals from the younger girls and the family's money. Anything she wants, she just takes. She has no friends and hangs on to her sisters and cannot play with anyone. She is emotionally still 3 to 4 years behind.

> C's little sister [seven years old] thinks I am too hard on her, that I blame her for everything and am not nice to C. Some of this is probably true. Her eleven year old sister, who has been picked on by C for years, is suspicious of her and gets angry at her and wishes she could act more grown up. Her older brother [he is 16] tolerates her, but doesn't care to be with her.

The mother characterized the changes in herself and her relations with her husband as follows:

> I have had problems in public, living with and explaining her behavior. Because I became too involved in C's problems, I had to try to go back to school and work part time as a librarian, to have something that was mine.

C's behavior has caused serious disagreement between us [her and her husband]. Much time has been spent arguing and blaming. We have had counselling since she was five and I have had two years of psychiatric help.

The father is more positive and optimistic. He did not mention C's stealing; he commented that the other children have come to understand personality problems as a result of having lived with C. At the end of the interview form, he wrote,

Of late it appears that our family has begun to mean more to her [C]. She is more loving and demonstrates this love by hugging. She is more interesting to talk to because she initiates conversation.

The mother concluded with the following observations.

I do not have the same feelings for C that I do for my biological kids. I was not aware of the pressure that would be placed on us when we adopted. Perhaps we were too optimistic. We thought we could cope. . . . I would not do it again—raising a medically handicapped Indian-black child.

The doctors are not optimistic that C will be able to live independently and manage her own life as an adult. Hospital personnel predict that she will have to live in a half-way house or in a supervised apartment.

Another family had two children born to them and then transracially adopted two sons and a daughter. They are bitter toward the adoption agency, which, they feel gave them incomplete and false information. The father wrote,

Our 12 year old son has serious emotional and behavioral problems that are affecting school, sibling, and marital relationships. We now know that the agency was dishonest with us about the child's origins, birth circumstances, early care, etc. We are more and more convinced that agencies took horrible advantage of families in several ways: (1) gave false, intentionally incomplete information or withheld information needed when parents did not push, and (2) moved children at inappropriate times and too frequently . . . . Far too much divorce and pain is occurring because of the failure of skilled services to be available for families in these circumstances.

The mother wrote,

The hardest thing in our adoption was the absence of information on our third adopted child and the lack of help in working him into the family. He'd been badly abused and still expects us to send him away. He begs for it. We have *never* threatened it, and we always reply, "You are a member of our family, no matter *what* you do, we still love you."

A similar situation prevailed in a family that adopted a black child who was twenty months old. By the age of twelve, he was described as "egocentric" and lacking friends. He causes problems between the parents and the other children and appears "spaced out." The parents blame the welfare department and the foster parents for not having told them about his problems. Knowing what they do now, the mother believes the child was badly treated in the foster home in which he was living prior to the adoption. She believes that the welfare agency did not do enough screening of the child before the placement. She writes about her twelve-year-old son: "He disregards even the most elementary social conventions, such as traffic lights; he will leave a mess and the other family members have to clean up after him." At the time of the interview, the parents were planning to send the boy to a private, in-residence school. "Maybe he will appreciate home when he is away," the mother concluded.

Another family had one child born to them and then adopted a black boy when he was three and a half years old. The parents have discovered that he is diabetic and has some brain damage and severe learning disabilities. The mother wrote that she needs ten times the energy she has to look after him. She feels that the time that she devotes to him is resented by their older son, who is fourteen, and their six-year-old daughter. The situation has resulted in marital strain. The parents do not know if the learning disability is genetic or if it was caused by the care he received in the foster home. They are bitter at the failure of the social worker to provide them with more information. The father's parents severed contact with the family for three and a half years when they adopted transracially. Even after some reconciliation, the grandparents are embarrassed by their black grandson and try to avoid his visiting them in their small community. In their interview, they emphasized that there are "really great problems in adopting an older child."

In 1974 another of the families adopted their second black daughter. They had adopted a black girl in 1969 and had two sons born to them. Prior to her adoption, B had lived in five different foster homes and had been adopted previously by a white family. She was removed from that home when the adoptive mother's condition was diagnosed as "borderline schizophrenic." The parents describe B as having no conscience. They claim that her experiences in five foster homes has "taught her how to survive." During the first year or so after this adoption, she used to wake up screaming in the middle of the night. She also has had seizures, which the parents attribute to past abuse. The two brothers have pleaded with their parents to send her back. The worst problem, however, exists between the first adopted daughter, K, who is ten years old, and B, who is eight. According to the mother,

K has troubles competing with B for attention. B knew all the tricks by the time she came to our family and infuriated K constantly. After five years, there is still jealousy and irritation on the part of K toward B.

At the end of the interview the mother commented,

I used to believe that environment was the dominant force in a person's life. Now I think you are born with a certain genetic character and that this remains pure and strong throughout life. Any changes that occur in a basic personality are really very minor. In other words, I think B could very well become a juvenile delinquent in spite of the influence living with us might have.

Another family adopted a five-year-old Korean boy who was fourteen at the time they completed their questionnaire. They hoped that the worst was over and that the last six months pointed the way to a brighter future. The mother wrote,

For a long time there have been problems, and I think we have partly gotten to the bottom of them by finding out over last summer that K has a learning disability. . . . And I think just knowing that he has this problem and attempting to understand it and work around it and having K know that he doesn't do as well in school as his sisters because of the learning disability and not because he's stupid has helped his self-image a great deal and has helped us in dealing with him. That's really the biggest problem. He has a few other personality traits that are difficult at times to live with. He was five years old when he came. There were things that are part of his personality that probably we may never undo. But the basic thing was the learning disability and also he occasionally will take things that do not belong to him. His sense of (I don't know how to put it) but if he wants it and can't see any other way of getting it, he will take it. And we have struggled long and hard to undo this and give him a better sense of what's right and wrong. We did have some counseling earlier this year last fall, and the outcome of that basically was that the counseling was not doing K a great deal of good because he did not see the reason for the counseling. However, I came out of the experience feeling a lot better about the job I was doing as mother. K can sometimes make me feel uncomfortable, and I think it makes his sisters feel uncomfortable too because, for some reason, his relationships with females have a sexual overtone. He does not either know how or distinguish platonic love from a sexual love. So this can put me on edge and other females that come in contact with him as well, especially since he's so young.

The experience of rearing her adopted son caused the mother to evaluate her roles and her commitment, and she expressed the results of that evaluation as follows.

The counseling was very helpful to me. I have a very strong conviction about my definition of a mother and what mothering is and because this is an adopted child—I don't know, I am not quite sure how to express it—but both of us, I think, T and I, are doing the very best that we can with this child. But should a time come when he is an adult and if he doesn't turn out perhaps as we would wish, that's okay. I think I will have the satisfaction of knowing that I did everything I could to help him be a reasonably responsible adult. We are still concerned about the fact that he takes things. Should there come a time—if we can't overcome this—when there will be a time when we cut loose and say, hey, we did the best we could, and that's it. Personality wise, I am absorbed in my children, I care about them, trying to do the very best we can, but they are not my whole life. I have another life besides the time and effort that I put into them that I find fulfilling. I haven't put all my eggs into one basket.

Even in the face of all the problems, strains and disappointments, both parents are optimistic about their relationship with K. They hope that K and his sisters will relate to each other with less tension and that the family will find peace together.

Scenario 3

The third scenario considers parents who feel guilt because they believe their decision to adopt transracially caused pain or harm to their biological child(ren). In one such family, the father commented that their oldest daughter has learned to repress her hostility toward her two younger adopted black siblings. "She has been taught that only bad people hate blacks or adopted children." This has resulted in some guilt and confusion. Their younger son, who was born to them, went through a period "of wanting to be black and adopted." The mother added that when the boy was five or six years old, he felt he was of "less value—because our social life revolved around the adoption and around a group of adopted parents." Shortly after they adopted the two children, the parents moved into a racially mixed neighborhood in order to help their adjustment.

Another family adopted a black girl who is now eight years old. Before the adoption, they had had a son who is now eleven years old. The mother felt that she had neglected her son out of concern for her daughter. She characterized the daughter as "hyperactive and in need of special care, attention and understanding." Of her son, she said that while "he understands her problem logically, it still causes resentment and makes him feel isolated." The mother also expressed concern about the fact that her adopted daughter was experiencing serious identity problems. She wrote, "I am white. I feel frustrated because I wish to encourage her positive blackness." She commented about herself, "I sometimes forget L's need to identify with a special heritage." She and her husband are confused about activities that might enhance L's awareness of her black heritage. They have no black friends, and L knows nothing about black history or culture. Concerning the future, the mother wrote, "L seems confused about her 'other' mother. We have explained adoption in terms of love and personal selection, but I, too, feel the need for L to eventually seek out her biological parents." This mother seems to feel less commitment to her adopted child. She is more tentative about her ties to her daughter than the other mothers.

While not exactly consistent with the characteristics of scenario 3, the following problem is sufficiently similar to be included. Both parents report that their adopted white daughter is jealous of her adopted brother's American Indian heritage. The mother wrote that the daughter "refuses to accept family or school rules, is generally negative, and resorts to name calling and tantrums." The family has participated in the activities of the local Native American Culture School. Their son has danced in Pow Wows. The father commented, "The opportunity to meet, get acquainted with, and ultimately to feel accepted as part of the local Native American Community has been wonderful. It has enriched all our lives." The last sentence does not quite mesh with the parents' earlier observations about their daughter's jealousy and sense of being left out.

A few other problems bear mentioning but do not quite fit scenarios 1, 2, or 3. The first involves a family with three children. The biological daughters are nine and five years old, and the oldest is an adopted, eleven-year-old black son. The mother describes him as having considerable problems. The father, on the other hand, claims "all is well." Conflicting reports from mothers and fathers are most unusual. In over 90 percent of the families, both parents saw eye-to-eye about their children. Some of the mother's concern is evident in the excerpt below:

> R gets hassled by black peers because he has white siblings and parents. His sisters get taunted in school by blacks, but their brother will not stand up for them. The sisters are confused by the blacks' anger at them. When we go downtown, R walks apart from us and tries to dissasociate himself from us to avoid hearing comments like "look at that nigger with white folks."

The mother anticipates that R will eventually reject both his parents and his siblings and will not consider them his family. The father does not mention any of this. He concentrates on R's superior performance in school and his high IQ. The father believes that R will remain a part of the family and predicts that he will live a life similar to their own. Both parents explained that after adopting R, they moved into a neighborhood that was at least 40 percent black. it is a low-income neighborhood, in which there is much black hostility toward whites. The mother concluded the interview by saying, "Things are hard, confusing, and disillusioning." She complained that she never expected such hostility. She said she used to feel that whites were responsible for racism but now she recognizes that racism is a "two-way street." "It is a lot harder than I expected." She believes that racial hostility and animosity will get worse. Her son and her whole family are caught in the middle. The father commented that the decision to adopt R and live in that neighborhood was more difficult for his wife than for him.

In another family situation, the mother expressed a resentment toward one of her adopted sons which was not shared by the father. There are seven children in the family, five of whom were born to the parents. They are now eighteen, seventeen, sixteen, fourteen, and twelve years of age. Two black sons, ages eleven and ten, were adopted. The mother wrote,

> I feel resentment toward this child [the 10 year old] because he has always rejected me. We don't trust each other. Everything we do is seen in a negative light. We don't communicate—I feel I have failed. I feel guilty and am disappointed in myself.[9]

She also wrote that their adopted son excels in school, has great interest in black history, and identifies strongly as black. The father's only reference to difficulties was: "There are some relationship problems in the triangle of mother, son, and father." He also told us that their decision to adopt a black child "had a tremendous effect on [his] wife's family. They cut her off entirely for three years."

About the future, he says, "We will move back into a mixed community before the two adopted boys are teenagers. I think it is a mistake to be in an all-white neighborhood."

Single-Parent Families

Of the 143 families who participated in our study, 19 sets of parents reported that they were divorced and 1 was separated. In 2 families, the fathers died, and in one family, both parents died. In the last instance, the two transracially adopted children are being reared by their older brother and sister. Thus 1 out of 6 of the families in our study are now single-parent families.

In the divorced families, 11 of the mothers and 2 of the fathers have custody of all the children.[10] In another 6 families, each parent has custody of at least one child. Of the mothers and fathers thirteen served as respondents. The relationship between those parents responding to our survey and those having custody is shown in table 3-2.

It is natural to expect the custodial parent to be the more likely to respond. However, one of the mothers and one of the fathers did not meet that expectation. In families in which the parents share custody, one might expect both parents to respond. But 4 of the mothers failed to do so, compared to 1

Table 3-2
Relationship between Parents Who Responded to Interview and Custody

Respondent	Custodial Mother	Custodial Father	Both	Combined
Mother	7	1[a]	1	9
Father	1	2	4	7
Both	3	—	1	4
Combined	11	3	6	20

[a]Separated.

of the fathers. The mother is the custodial parent of all or some of the children in 17 families, and she is the sole or joint respondent in 13 questionnaires. The father has custody of some or all of the children in 9 families and is the sole or joint respondent in 11 questionnaires. The relationships between custody and respondent suggest that the noncustodial fathers have not walked away from their children. The fact that they have taken the time to complete the questionnaire must be viewed as evidence of their commitment.[11]

Each of our 20 families have at least 2 children, 1 of whom was adopted transracially. Children were already born to 18 of the families before they adopted. There is a total of 2 to 6 children in each family.

The fathers have custody of the children in 3 of the single-parent families; 2 are divorced, and 1 couple is separated. In the last family, the mother responded to our questionnaire. It is a family of 4 children, 2 adopted transracially. They are both described as "mixed, black and white." The son identifies as black, the daughter as white. The mother said that relations among all the children and between children and parents are basically positive and good. She also said that the separation was not related to the adoption or to the children in any way. The adoption has made her life richer and has given her more self-confidence, both in a personal sense and in her professional role as a teacher.

In the other 2 families in which the father has sole custody, he was also the respondent. In 1 family, the father has custody of 4 children, 2 of whom were transracially adopted. At the time of the interview, one of the adopted black sons was nine, the other eleven years old. The 2 daughters born into the family are older. One attends a Catholic high school, the other is in eighth grade at a Catholic school. The father believes relationships among all members of the family are basically good. Apart from reading, there has been less time since the divorce for the family to engage in activities to enhance the adopted children's racial background. They live in an all-white neighborhood, the adopted children identify as white, their close friends are white, and the father expects that when they grow up they will want to live in the same type of community. He wrote that the transracial adoption was not specifically involved in the divorce, but "four kids were too much for my former wife." About changes in his own personality, he said that the adoption "increased his awareness and sensitivity to discrimination to blacks and others, including women."

There are 5 children in the other family headed by a custodial father. An eight-year-old black son was adopted transracially. This father has remarried a woman who teaches at a black school. In response to the question on family activities, the father related that his wife's teaching at a black school has provided opportunities to expose his son to black situations: "The family is affirming my son's blackness." The father believes that in the past, his son's blackness was less important than it should have been. He views the transracial adoption as a positive factor in his second marriage.

In both of these families, the fathers are positive about their relations with their children and about their decisions to adopt transracially. They are not "problem families."

The 11 families in which the mothers have custody may also be rated as generally positive. The mothers (and the fathers, in 4 instances in which both parents responded) wrote that relations are basically positive and good. In 3 of the 7 families in which the mothers were the sole respondents, the women expressed bitterness toward their former husbands, claiming that they "rejected (their) children" (both those adopted and those born to them) and "ran away" from the responsibilities of 3 to 5 children. One mother said, "I think M got scared of the idea of five kids: not their races or the fact they were adopted—just that there were so many. He separated himself from us emotionally." That mother continued,

> Most of our problems and joys have to do with being a family, not a multiracial family, just a family. There's a lot of love and a lot of fun to go along with the problems mentioned above.
>
> A lot of our problems now are due to their father's rejection of them. His excuses for not seeing them (he lives two miles away) are thinner all the time. They all distrust him—and to an extent—all men. That's tough to handle. The six of us (there are five daughters, three adopted, two black, one Korean, and two born into the family) are in family counseling and its invaluable. It has helped bring us closer.

Another husband left his family after his wife, a biological daughter, and an adopted black son moved in with a black family. About her relations with her spouse, she wrote,

> The adoption probably had a negative effect on my husband. He wanted to be the only kid anyway. Any children would have had a similar effect. It's a wonder we got past the adoption agency. Though I'm a better mother now, I would probably never qualify to adopt now.[12]

She and her two children have lived with a black family in a neighborhood that is mostly black for a year. She described their experience as follows.

> Both mothers are mothers to all the kids. The black mother has helped care for B [her adopted son]. She has provided a black mother image for B.

She explained that some of her black friends worried if "our black son would be okay with white parents." She is proud, however, that "after one and a half years, the black mother called me an honorary black." About her own parents, she wrote, "My parents are WASP-type conservatives. They have never acknowledged their racism." Her son is in second grade. He gets along well with everyone. He considers himself "dark." About her own relations with him, she said,

> The slight problems I have are related to his sex role. He sees women on earth to serve him. He learned from his father. He bitches about helping around the house and expects me to serve him.

One custodial mother (and sole respondent) of two transracially adopted children commented about their decision to adopt a black son and daughter, who are now fifteen and sixteen years old:

> I'm not sure I would have adopted had I known I would be a single parent. I think I have grown mostly from the divorce, rather than from the trans-racial adoption. I'm unsure whether the adoption had any effect on our decision to divorce. My husband seemed threatened by kids.

The father served as respondent from another family in which the mother has custody of their two sons (one adopted black son and one born to them). He wrote,

> Our divorce really centered on non-child factors. My former wife wanted a single career, especially a career in another part of the country. My former wife and I are both persons who have pretty clear ideas about who we are and what our goals are and I think that fact more than racial factors has resulted in our boys being secure, open people. They've gone through a divorce and a major move, and they still seem to be full of fun and open to life. The interracial families I've seen which have had problems are the ones where the parents feel guilty about being white and overcompensated. Those kids often seem to have identity problems. I think children need parents and they don't care about the color of those parents.

About his adopted nine-year-old son he said,

> He is doing well in school, has many friends, and his mother tells me she has no special problems with him. He considers himself black, but most of

his friends are white. My guess is that he'll marry a white girl mostly because he has a "liberated" mother and is growing up in a white culture. If he marries a black girl, I would guess she would be from a middle-class home with a successful mother.

Among three sets of parents in which the mother has custody of the children, both parents completed the interviews. In reviewing them, we found the mother and father to be in agreement about the relationships between parents and children and between the adopted children and their siblings who were born into the families. In each family, both parents believed that relations were basically positive and good. None of the parents related the divorce to the transracial aspect of the adoption, but they did relate the divorce to the presence of children.

One mother wrote that her former husband seemed unable to accept their younger adopted son for who he was. She claimed that the father's high regard for academic achievement made it difficult for him to accept the child, who has a learning disability. "It got in the way of our marriage." The mother also wrote that she has a better relationship with her two adopted sons (ages ten and eleven) than she has with the two sons that she bore (ages twelve and sixteen). The father in that family claimed that the divorce was unrelated either to the adoption or to children. He did, however, discuss his closeness to the oldest adopted son. He said he had an easier time maintaining the father-son relationship with him than with any of the other children during the divorce.

In another of the families where both parents responded, the custodial mother wrote that the divorce was unrelated to the adoption or to the children. The father, however, said, they [he and his spouse] had had problems sharing love and disagreed about disciplining the children.

The third group of single-parent families includes those in which each parent has custody of at least 1 child. There are 6 such families, each numbering 2 to 6 children. In 4 of the families, the biological and adopted sons live with their fathers. In the other 2 families, both sons and daughters live with their fathers. In 5 of the families, the biological and adopted daughters live with their mothers. In 1 family, the biological and adopted sons live with their mother. There is some tendency toward unisex households, and gender seems to be more important than race in deciding who lives with whom. None of the children are preschoolers, and age does not appear to be a factor.

None of the divorced mothers has remarried; 5 of the fathers have. One of those fathers has custody of all the children, and 2 of them have custody of some of the children. None of our interviews indicated that the living and custody arrangements were dictated by any outside persons or insititutions. In a few instances, the respondents explained why or how they made the choices they did.

In one particular family, the father has the 2 adopted sons (one white, one black) and the daughter lives with her biological mother. The father explained, "A has decided to live with her mother partly because she doesn't want to live with N her adopted brother." Speaking of his 2 sons, the father said, "V communicates very little with me or with other adults. N is presently testing rules both at home and in school. The boys also attack each other if they are at home together for very long." Although the father said "I believe we would have separated if we had not adopted the child," he also said that the adoption increased the strain between his wife and him.

In another family the adopted black daughter and a biological son live with the father, while the other biological son lives with the mother. The father explained, "B had problems relating to her mother. She does not visit often." Both of these fathers acknowledge on-going problems with the adopted children, but they also note that divorce has alleviated some of the tensions.

In the family in which the mother has custody of their two adopted black daughters and the father has custody of their two biological sons, the mother identified strongly with her adopted daughters. She wrote, "Their mannerisms, behavior, and attitudes toward life are similar to mine. Looking at them is like looking at myself. What affects them now, greatly affected me." About her former spouse and their two biological sons, she wrote, "He left us and married a younger teenage girl. They moved into a white suburb with our two bio-sons and live an upwardly mobile traditional life."

In the family with 6 children (5 of whom were transracially adopted sons), the father has custody of 3 sons and the 1 biological daughter. The mother has custody of 2 adopted sons. The father offered no explanation for their living arrangement, and the age of the children does not seem to have been a factor. We characterized all the children as being healthy emotionally and physically. He wrote,

> I am very happy with my family and would adopt the children again. The children, in turn, feel good about themselves and are happy. I do not feel that the fears of genocide or loss of racial identity voiced by those opposed to transracial adoption a few years ago mean much now and certainly will not in the future. I believe transracial adoption is an alternative to resolving foster care or permanent institutionalization. Whatever problems these children will face in their lives, will be better faced with the support of a family, even if it is white.

Thus in all of the divorced families, the children appear to have no *more* problems than the children in families that are intact. Occasionally we sense bitterness on the part of one of the spouses (more often the mother than the the father). But even in those families, the mothers do not claim that the father's leaving has caused problems for the children. The issue of having adopted transracially seems unimportant and irrelevant.

We turn finally to the three families in which one or both parents have died. In the family that lost both parents, the two transracially adopted girls live with their older brother and sister. The sister is the children's legal guardian. The father died several years before the mother. She died shortly before the 1979 survey. The sister characterized her relationship with the children as basically positive and good. "They seem to be dealing with our mother's death." The sister believes the girls are well integrated in their school, neighborhood, and way of life. They identify themselves as "mixed." Most of their friends are white. They have started to date, and most of the boys are white. The sister expects that race will not be an important factor in their choice of community or spouse.

Of the other two families, one of the fathers died in 1971, leaving his wife and 4 children. The 2 biological children have married and are no longer living at home. The transracially adopted son and daughter still at home are both black. The mother wrote, "Basically we have a very good situation. Our daughter identifies as black; our son, who is light skinned, as white." They live in a white neighborhood, and their friends are white. At the end of the interview, the mother explained that she plans to move into a more integrated neighborhood when her daughter gets older, so that she can have black friends. The mother feels that she has had more than her share of tragedy, losing her husband when the children were so young. She goes on to say that with the knowledge of hindsight, she would make the same decision again. "Our family is close, and we all have a good feeling about each other."

There is a special sense of poignancy about the second family. The father died in 1978, leaving his wife and their eleven-year-old black adopted daughter. The mother believes that the child has been deeply hurt by her father's death. She tries to relate to her daughter as a parent and as a close and intimate friend. In describing the changes in her own personality, the mother observed, "I am stronger, less self-centered and have a much richer life. My grieving and ability start toward a new life have been speeded up by my loving daughter and her needs."

The mother and daughter live in an all-white suburb, and the daughter identifies herself as black. They are exploring African history, art, and culture. At the end of the questionnaire, the mother wrote about planning trips, shopping, walks, bird watching, and so on together. More than any of the other single-parent families, this mother seems to *need* her adopted daughter (her only child) and to derive happiness from her. The mother perceives their relationship as one of great intimacy and joy.

Blessed Families

The 10 blessed families perceive themselves as special in the most positive sense. One set of parents used such phrases as ''a stewardship from God'' to describe their black nine-year-old daughter. Another parent told us that their black adopted son ''has brought talent, strength, and physical beauty to this family that were not to be produced from our own genes.'' A family with 4 biological sons describes their adopted black daughter as a ''gift.''

These ultrapositive families exhibit no special demographic characteristics that set them apart. The numbers of children in the 10 families range from 1 to 8: One family has only 1 child, an adopted Eskimo daughter; 2 others have 2 adopted black sons each; another has 3 adopted children, a white son, and 2 daughters, one white, the other black. The other 6 families have either 4 children each, in which one or two have been adopted; 5 children, in which one or two are adopted; and, in one family, there are 8 children, 6 of whom have been adopted. Nor do the parents' ages, religious affiliations, and/or professional training distinguish them from the others. The fathers' occupations include salesman, engineer, lawyer, aircraft mechanic, and educator. The mothers are all housewifes. Three of the families report that their neighborhoods are racially mixed; the others describe them as mostly white with a few blacks, Orientals, or American Indians.

In 7 of the 10 families, the parents perceive their adopted children as having strong and positive identifications with their respective racial groups. The children identify themselves as black or Indian or Eskimo even though most of their friends are white. However, 3 children from 3 different families contradict this perception: One Indian child considers herself white; and 2 black children who have light skins consider themselves mixed or white.

The experiences reported by these parents about relations with grandparents, aunts, uncles, and so on are similar to those of the other families. For some, the grandparents were initially opposed to the adoption but eventually relented. For most, there were no problems. The children have been and are accepted as members of the extended family. One mother wrote,

> Our daughter has enriched all of our lives, aunts and uncles, too, many times over. One of the grandparents began with a very skeptical or belligerent attitude. It was wonderful to see him become just as warm and friendly as he was to all his grandchildren.

. Some common and overwhelming themes emerge from these blessed families: They are committed to transracial adoption; they believe in the value of mixing and integrating persons of different races; and they share a sense that their roles as parents of black children has wrought a profound change in their own personalities and identities. A mother who has 2 adopted black sons and no biological children, said,

> I am no longer white, nor do I think of my family as only white. My reactions are like that of a black. I can relate to blacks much more easily than to white liberals on racial issues. We are no longer a white family, but a mixed family.

In another family with 5 children, in which 3 are adopted black sons and 1 an adopted black daughter, the mother wrote, "I have a whole new perception of the world. We say to the children, if we go into a restaurant, 'We're the only people in here who aren't white.' " About her relations with her husband, she wrote, "By adopting visibly different children, we have made a statement, a real commitment. There is a tightness between us, a special supportiveness, we need each other." Another mother with 4 biological sons and a younger adopted black daughter wrote,

> I do consider her a gift to us, but that is the way all children should be considered. I hope she and all the boys will be blessed some similar way in their lives. In my heart I grieve that there has been antagonism to transracial adoption. I feel its basis is fear and it may lessen in time. Subsidizing black, or for that matter white, couples who want a child very much may be one answer. I hope it works. Would that by itself though take care of the number of children that need a home? I still cannot see that one's culture comes before a caring and loving situation for any child.

These families do not place special emphasis on rituals or activities to enhance the adopted child's awareness or identity with his or her racial background. A father wrote, "We probably don't do enough of this. Our neglect isn't ideological but due mostly to plain inertia." Another mother said, "We always hope to do more than we do. Time goes by too fast. Two years ago, we went to hear Alex Haley speak." On the other hand, the father of a family that had 3 sons before they adopted an American black daughter and a Vietnamese black daughter, told us,

> There are some things that can't be faked. There is no way we can give them (our daughters) the "black experience," whatever that is. For me, these adoptions have been a blessing. I have never once regretted our decision to adopt and I hope that we are able to give them the mental toughness they undoubtedly will need to cope with a racial conscious society. Rightly or wrongly. I don't think of these girls as my racially mixed adopted daughters. To me they are simply my daughters and I am afraid all of these studies and probings in racial adoptions have a slightly dehumanizing effect on all of us, however well intentioned.

The children themselves are the most consistent factors linking these families. None of the parents report brain damage, a history of emotional or physical abuse, personality problems, drug or alcohol abuse, or stealing. All the parents reported that their adopted children are good to excellent students. Three of the families described their adopted children as "gifted." The parents who had adopted a baby Eskimo girl said, "E is an excellent student. She's gifted in language, art, gymnastics," In another family in which an adopted black daughter is the fourth child and the only girl, the parents wrote, "She does very well in school, she is at the top of her class, she plays three instruments, likes to do handiwork, is good at math and can knit. Perhaps she will become a lawyer like her father." Another mother said of her adopted black son:

> He is an excellent student. He has extraordinary physical coordination and strength. He also draws like a young Matisse. His teacher wrote on his report card "V is such an interesting combination of talent—it is a pleasure to know and teach him." V is a happy, self-confident and very talented person who finds his own way.

About the future—where the adopted child will live and with whom he or she will identify—these parents responded as most of the others did. For the most part, they still think it is too early to give an informed opinion, but they guess that their adopted children are likely to emulate their families' life style. They will live middle and upper-middle-class lives in communities in which white people are sympathetic to mixed racial groups. Sentiments such as the following were expressed:

> I feel as though they will live mostly in the community in which they have been raised because this is where they feel at home. I would not object if they would seek out a black community. I doubt they will!

A mother said,

> I want my black children to find black partners, I want them to believe that black is beautiful, and I want them to experience that in dating and in marriage.

Two of the families have traveled a good deal. In one family, the husband and wife lived in Africa for 2 years before they had children. Their home is filled with African artifacts. The mother said, "I am no longer white and do not think of my family as white." Another set of parents reported that they have traveled together to Africa, Eastern Europe, and Mexico. At home they have many friends from different racial backgrounds, and there is often much discussion about different cultures around the world.

In a third family, the oldest son (biological) spent a summer living with a native family in Thailand. The father described his son's experiences at the local school, learning to speak Thai, and observing the social and religious customs: "[They] were as entirely different from his own as the breakfast menu of boiled morning glories and rice." Internationalism and cosmopolitanism are important themes for these families.

One of the mothers, an adoptee herself, had searched for her biological parents. Now, as an adoptive mother, she is particularly sensitive to her daughter's anticipated desires. She is the same mother who said,

> I find myself more involved in E's activities than I'd ever thought possible. Much of my life has been devoted to sitting on a bench watching her ice skate these past three years.

This account of a mother's involvement in her child's life and activities is not typical of the group as a whole. However, in none of the other families is the adopted child an only child. Their accounts do not describe such concentrated devotion and attention to the interests and activities of their adopted children.

Families Who Did Not Respond

Ten families did not respond to the survey, but neither did they explicitly refuse to be interviewed. When we did not receive their questionnaires in the mail, we contacted them by phone. At that point they told us they would rather complete their questionnaires than do the interview by phone. None of them did. A review of these families' 1972 survey responses does not indicate any pattern of characteristics that distinguishes them from the 93 percent who did participate in the second survey.

Their demographic characteristics differed in no systematic manner from the rest of the families. The fathers' occupations included university professor, minister (2), skilled laborer, engineer (3), self-employed (2), and social worker. All but two of the mothers had stopped working outside the home after the birth or adoption of their first child. One of the working mothers was a university professor, the other was a graduate student. The mothers' ages ranged from twenty-seven to thirty-nine years; the fathers' from twenty-nine to forty-nine years. Three of the families had adopted all their children: One adopted two boys (one black, one white) and a Korean girl. The other 7 families each had at least 1 biological child before they adopted. The largest family consisted of 1 adopted and 3 biological children. The adopted children among the 7 families were either American black or Korean. Five of the families said that they were planning or considering at least one more transracial adoption.

In 3 of the 10 families, grandparents had disapproved of the adoptions, and relationships were strained or severed. The parents discussed this with a sense of bitterness.

One of the families was experiencing serious problems at the time of the first survey. It was a family in which both parents were professionally trained, and both had been married before. Their only children were two adopted daughters of Mexican background. The younger one was black-haired and dark, and the older one was blond and fair. The older daughter was five in 1972 and was seeing a psychotherapist four times a week. Her problems took the form of wild, uncontrollable crying and temper tantrums. She was also physically and verbally abusive toward her younger sister, who was then two years old. The parents told us in 1972 that the arrival of the second child (at age four months) had triggered wild, angry behavior on the part of their older daughter, who was three at the time.

The parents did not seem bitter. They did not claim they had been led astray by the social worker or adoption agency or that crucial information had been kept from them. Nor did they indicate that they felt the adoption had been a mistake. There were no signs of diminished commitment from either the father or the mother. Their child had a severe problem. This family probably faced a long and difficult road. When asked for the advice they might offer other families considering transracial adoption, the mother stressed the importance of family involvement in the adopted child's culture. She offered no warnings about the dangers of physical or emotional disturbances.

Another set of parents (the mother especially) became "radicalized" and sympathetic toward the position of black social workers. They told us in 1972 that they would discourage white families from adopting black children and that they favored a policy that would make transracial adoptions illegal. The parents explained that they did not believe a white family could rear a black child and give him a sense of black culture. They emphasized that they had acquired these beliefs in the past few years, after having adopted their seven-year-old black son at the age of nine months. They also had an eight-year-old son who had been born to them.

With the exception of the last two families (one in which a daughter was in therapy and one in which the parents came to oppose transracial adoption morally), none of the 10 demonstrate any signs by which we could have predicted that they would fail to complete the second phase. None of their experiences were particularly negative or extremely disturbing. As a group, they appear much like the other 133 families who did respond to the follow-up study.

Notes

1. The families received the more recent questionnaire and talked to us by phone. Most of them promised to complete and return the questionnaire, but none did so.

2. Alfred Kadushin, *Adopting Older Children* (Columbia University Press, New York, 1970).

3. Lucille J. Grow and Deborah Shapiro, *Black Children—White Parents: A Study of Transracial Adoption* (Child Welfare League of America, New York, 1974).

4. Ibid., p. iii.

5. Ibid., p. 103.

6. A few of the families learned later that their adopted child had physical problems. One was born with a congenital heart problem; the other suffers from petit mal epilepsy. Nevertheless, they felt very positive about their decision to adopt and about their experiences with their daughters. At the end of the interview schedule, one of those mothers wrote,

> The girls [aged 4 and 11, black/white] brought a totally new element into our sterile lives, first because of adoption, then because of race. They [adopted daughters] made our biological children [two sons, 12 and 14 years old] more aware of the stupidity of prejudice. They opened up a whole new world, that we could not have known any other way. There has been very positive growth in our sons and in us. I would certainly recommend transracial adoption. Thank God we have all four kids.

7. Grow and Shapiro, *Black Children*, p. 102.

8. A profile of that family is provided in Rita Simon and Howard Altstein, *Transracial Adoption* (Wiley Interscience, New York, 1977), pp. 80-92.

9. In rereading the mother's 1972 interview when the child was three years old (he had been adopted when he was seven months), we found that the mother had said then that he preferred his dad to her and that she resented this. She had also said he seemed fearful of her.

10. In the family that was separated at the time of the interview, the children were living with their father in the family home.

11. The ease or lack of ease in locating either of the parents does not explain the proportion of mothers and fathers who responded.

12. The respondent is probably referring to the fact that she is pregnant and her boyfriend is planning to move into her apartment, though she does not mention marriage plans.

Part II
The Debate Continues: Pro and Con Transracial Adoption

4

Arguments and Organizations: Pro, Con, and Neutral

Introduction

Between 1975 and 1980, the public positions on transracial adoption assumed by both nonwhite (especially black) and white organizations became increasingly polarized. Opponents have argued that the process represents a white plot to brainwash a generation of blacks; or an attempt by white females to use black male children to substitute for their inability to interact with black male adults.[1] However, these pronouncements are becoming more muted. Terms such as "diabolical trick," "a form of genocide," "one of the many conspiracies being waged against black people, " and "fulfilling a rescue fantasy"[2] are now rarely heard.

Transracial adoption has been regarded as an insult to the strength of the black family, an institution that some claim has been historically weakened by whites.[3] Opponents argue that transracial adoption would never have existed if white-operated child-welfare agencies had recognized the potential for adoption within black families.[4] An increasing sense of awareness has become more prevalent among black leaders: rhetoric alone, regardless of issue, will not right historic injustices. Sloganeering on this issue, as on others, has given way to collective action to implement political goals. For blacks, the issues involved in transracial adoption include a wide array of political, social, economic, and psychological grievances.

The extent of the problem of adoptable children can be appreciated by the following figures. In 1978 approximately 500,000-750,000 children lived in out-of-home placements. About 102,000 of these children were legally free for adoption, and 49 percent of them were eleven years or older. Approximately 28 percent of the available children were black, and another 10 percent were Hispanic, Oriental, Native American, and "other."[5] The majority of children most available for adoption will probably not be adopted.

In 1975, the last year for which Department of Health, Education and Welfare (HEW) figures are available, 104,188 children were adopted. Black children constituted 11 percent of those adoptions (11,400 children). Transracial adoptions numbered 831, accounting for about 0.08 percent of the total number of children adopted. If the 1975 transracial adoption rate had continued into 1978 or even increased slightly, it would have had little effect on increasing the number of nonwhite children placed. The greatest number of transracial adoptions occurred in 1971, and even then there were only 2,574 such placements.

Neutral or On-the-Fence Groups

National Associations of Social Workers

The National Association of Social Workers (NASW) is the largest of the social-work organizations and the one to which most professional social workers belong. NASW creates and maintains professional standards and policies and supports relevant legislation.

Proposals from individual chapters are considered by the Delegate Assembly, which meets every two years. Proposals must be approved by a board of directors before they are presented. In 1977 the Colorado Chapter offered the following statement for consideration by the Delegate Assembly:

> The often limited resources in adoptive placements for minority and minority-mixed children must be recognized. Special efforts should be made to place children in need of permanent homes in homes of like racial background to that of the child's biological parents. . . .[6]

The Colorado delegation wanted to call attention to the issue of the availability of adoptable nonwhite children and the relative scarcity of prospective nonwhite adoptors.

But the statement has implications beyond its intent. If it were intended simply to call attention to the lack of potential minority adoptive homes, it would seem to oppose transracial adoption. It does not mention children who, for whatever reason, cannot be placed "in homes of like racial background to that of [their] biological parents. . . ."

Several months after the Delegate Assembly met in 1977, it approved certain of the *Actions and Resolutions*. No mention of transracial adoption was made in the section on "Families and Children," nor in that entitled, "Policy on Family and Children." The only statement faintly relevant to transracial adoption was,

> Children have a right to permanent family ties, primarily of which is the natural family. No child should be denied the opportunity for a permanent, nurturing family environment because of lack of services or lack of financial resources.[7]

In 1979 the following statement was included for consideration by the Delegate Assembly in the section, "Public Policy/Adoption,"

Recruitment of adoptive parents from each relevant ethnic or racial group should be aggressively pursued to meet the needs of children who require placement.

In their final statement, the NASW still avoided direct discussion of transracial adoption.

Children's agencies must mount aggressive attacks on the barriers that have traditionally, and often still remain, in the way of achieving permanent homes for children. . . , theoretical barriers, unsupported by test experience, such as resistance to utilizing single parents, foster parents and non-traditional family patterns as potential adoption sources.[8]

Nontraditional family patterns do not necessarily relate to transracial placement, as these are traditional family settings. If not for the unsubstantiated and often emotional rhetoric surrounding transracial adoption, it would probably have been included as a "non-traditional family pattern."

Even though most of the 1979 Delegate Assembly's *Actions on Adoption and Foster Care* do not leave the way open to transracial adoption as an alternative, the term itself was not used. The Delegate Assembly recognized that:

Various socio-cultural changes, the growth of new attitudes, major changes in the adoption population, and indications of new research findings have substantially altered the face of adoption, yet broad policy and practice developments have not kept pace. . . .

Many children remain "lost" in the system and are subject to its worst effects. . . . A greater attempt needs to be made to rationally relate these two systems [foster-care and adoption] to each other and to the general welfare services available to families and their children, thereby affording the widest possible range of alternatives and providing an integrated approach to meeting needs.

The social work profession . . . has a responsibility to assist in assessing public social policy with regard to [foster-care and] adoption, to ensure that it reflects the best and most current knowledge in the field, and that it consistently meets the needs of children and of the community . . . ongoing research and evaluation should inform and guide policy and practices in adoption [and foster-care].[9]

Clearly, transracial adoption is related to these issues. If "ongoing research and evaluation should inform and guide policy and practices in adoption," then it behooves child-placement agencies to examine the extensive data available on transracial adoption and draw the necessary conclusions. Most of the data indicate that it is an effective method of achieving permanent placement for children. Even the most skeptical must admit that transracial adoption is within societal standards as an alternative when inracial adoptive parents are not available.

Even though it would appear to be particularly applicable, transracial adoption is not mentioned in the Delegate Assembly's concluding remarks in *Actions on Adoption*:

> Special attention should be given to the needs of so-called hard-to-place children (including older children, racially mixed children, physically, mentally or emotionally handicapped), with particular care applied to *insure protection of their right to a caring environment.*[10]

All data indicate that parents adopt transracially because they genuinely want to have a child. The best way to implement the NASW statement, "to insure protection of [a child's] right to a caring environment," would be simply to suggest transracial adoption to selected prospective adoptive couples. This addresses a fundamental issue raised by nonwhite opponents of transracial adoption: that it came into being because adoption agencies failed to recruit nonwhite adoptive parents.

Paradoxically, transracial adoption is much less controversial and nontraditional than some other types of placement endorsed by the NASW. In testimony before the Advisory Committee for the White House Conference on Families, the NASW Executive Director recently stated,

> In our rush to idealize the family and strengthen it, we cannot diminish the rights and needs of persons who do not belong to families. . . . Public policies must be concerned with a public perspective which supports contemporary evolving family forms. . . . It would be useful to have new research on the working definitions [of the family] already in use, formally and informally, by institutions and government agencies at all levels.[11]

In referring to "the rights and needs of persons who do not belong to families," the executive director spoke not only on behalf of new family patterns but echoed a historic social work principle: self-determination. This supports an individual's right to behave or to have a life style of his/her own choosing, so long as it is not detrimental to others. In child-welfare and particularly foster-care practice, social work encourages the concept of self-determination for the benefit of the children. For example, in 1979, the New Jersey Department of Human Services acknowledged that for four years it had been carefully placing homosexual adolescents in lesbian-headed foster homes: "Some heterosexual foster parents just can't deal with the kinds of problems these kids have."[12] The head of the influential North American Center on Adoption (to be discussed later in this chapter) cautiously endorsed this unique program.

An assistant to the New Jersey Human Services Commissioner stated that social workers found in these homosexual homes, "No indication that a gay foster parent is more likely to sexually abuse a child than a heterosexual foster parent."[13] (It had been suspected that these environments supported sexual abuse.)

Child Welfare League of America

The Child Welfare League of America was established 60 years ago. It is a privately supported organization of about 400 sectarian and nonsectarian, private and public child-welfare agencies. Its primary function is to "set standards and improve practice in all social services for children."[14] In attempting to adhere to these standards, the league has tried to walk the fine line between the opposing camps around transracial adoption.[15] To avoid the politics of the issue, it has recommended standards that are ambiguous and confusing. According to 1978 *Standards for Adoption Service* (SAS), the league's most recent position tried to be all things to all people;

> No standards of practice can be considered final; in one sense, the moment they are issued, they are out of date.[16]

> The primary purpose of an adoption service should be to help children who would not otherwise have a home of their own, and who can benefit from family life. . . .[17]

> The opportunity to have a permanent family should not be denied a child by reason of age, religion, race, nationality, residence. . . .[18]

> It is preferable to place a child in a family of his own racial background.[19]

> Consideration of adoptive parents of other races, however, is one of the means of achieving timely and needed permanence for children. . . . Every opportunity should be used to find a permanent home for a child awaiting adoptive placement.[20]

Thus the 1978 SAS reflects the league's ambivalence toward transracial adoption as a form of permanent placement for nonwhite children. The league views inracial adoption as the most desirable course but recognizes transracial adoption as an appropriate alternative.

The idea of racial differences between parent and child is somewhat discomforting for many and challenges our society's emphasis on the family as *the* arena for children's development. Under the SAS subtitle, "Suitability for Each Other" (that is, child and parent), the league states:

> Similarities of background or characteristics should not be a major consideration in the selection of a family, unless integration of the child into the family and the child's identification with them may be facilitated by a particular likeness *such as color*. (Authors' emphasis)[21]

> The adoptive parents selected for a child should ordinarily be of a similar racial background, but children should not have adoption denied or significantly delayed when adoptive parents of other races are available.[22]

Like other child-welfare groups, the league places greatest emphasis on the value of the nuclear family.

Arguments against Transracial Adoption

Most black writers opposed to transracial adoption challenge two main hypotheses:

1. There are insufficient black adoptive parents willing to adopt black children.
2. The benefits a black child will receive in a white family surpass those received in an institution.

They observe that many potential nonwhite adoptive parents are disqualified because of adoption agencies' widespread use of white, middle-class criteria for selection. They also observe that blacks historically have adopted informally, preferring not to rely on agencies and courts for sanction. Therefore, the figures cited by agencies cannot reflect the actual number of black adoptions. They feel that no longitudinal outcome data are available to show that transracial adoption of black children outweighs the known disadvantages of an institution or foster care.

Opponents of transracial adoption predict family and personal problems as the children grow into preadolescence and adolescence. A leading black organization points to transracially adopted black children being returned to foster care because the adoption was not "working out," or being placed in residential treatment by their white adoptive parents because they could not manage them.[23]

Amuzie Chimuzie, an opponent of transracial adoption, attributed "all consciously motivating human actions [for example, transracial adoption] (to) . . . selfish needs."[24] He has put forth an interesting but difficult suggestion. Recognizing that young children are rarely consulted when a major decision is to be made in their lives, he argues that this powerlessness is exacerbated for a young black child in a white adoptive family. Chimuzie suggests,

It seems appropriate that blacks collectively as parents should speak for the black child in matters touching transracial adoption. . . . It is up to the agent of the child—in this instance blacks as a group—to accept or reject it [transracial adoption]. . . . [I]t has not been determined whether a majority of the blacks are for or against transracial adoption of black children.

At the time Chimuzie wrote (1975), there was indeed only scant information on black attitudes toward transracial adoption. A 1971 survey of 100 persons indicated that blacks were split about evenly in their attitudes toward transracial adoption. Opponents were concerned about the eventual racial identity of the children, the "real" motivation of white families, and the fact that agencies were placing greater emphasis on locating white rather than black families.[25]

In 1977 Howard, Royce, and Skerl published the results of a survey of 150 black households.[26] Surprisingly, they found that 57 percent of the blacks surveyed had an "open" attitude (that is, they did not dislike and did not strongly object to transracial adoption). Seven percent were "most unfavorable" (that is, they disliked and strongly objected to transracial adoption). Three fourths of the individuals agreed that if no black home were available for an adoptable black child, "a white home might be beneficial." Sixteen percent did not agree.

Approximately one half of the participants felt that fewer difficulties would develop as a result of transracial adoption than from other nonpermanent placements such as institutional or foster care. Seventy-nine percent indicated that liberal white parents would be qualified to raise a black child if they gave up some of their white culture in order to give the child a chance to develop some black identity.

Perhaps one of the most important findings of the Howard study is revealed in table 4-1. Measurements were based on responses to the statement, "I would prefer a child being adopted by whites to having him/her lingering in a foster home or institution."

Howard's survey shows that many blacks, a majority of their sample, are not hostile to transracial adoption, and under certain conditions, most would support it. More than 80 percent indicated a preference for transracial adoption when the only other alternative would be an institution or a foster home. Only 14 percent found transracial adoption entirely unacceptable. While the child's ultimate racial identity was a concern, the need for a child to be accepted and loved appeared overriding. These data do not support the views of militant black individuals and organizations against transracial adoption.

One of the most prevalent arguments against transracial adoption is

Table 4-1
Cross-Tabulation of Preference for Transracial Adoptions over Other Alternatives, by Attitude toward Transracial Adoptions

Prefer Transracial Adoptions to Alternatives	Attitude toward Transracial Adoptions				
	Open	Confused	Somewhat Unfavorable	Most Unfavorable	Combined
Agree	90.6	88.5	58.6	40.0	80.7
	(77)	(23)	(17)	(4)	(121)
Do not know	4.7	3.8	6.9	10.0	5.3
	(4)	(1)	(2)	(1)	(8)
Disagree	4.7	7.7	34.5	50.0	14.0
	(4)	(2)	(1)	(5)	(21)
Total	100.0	100.0	100.0	100.0	100.0
	(85)	(26)	(29)	(10)	(150)

Note: Figures in parentheses indicate the number of respondents.

that while families, no matter how liberal or well intended, cannot teach a black child how to survive in an essentially racist society. Nonwhites opposed to transracial adoption insist that because white adoptive parents are not black and cannot experience nonwhite status, they are raising a psychologically defenseless individual, incapable of understanding and dealing with the racism that exists in our society. Amuzie Chimuzie articulates that position when he emphasizes the fears that black social workers and other experts in the child-rearing field have that black children reared in white homes will not develop the characteristics needed to survive and flourish in a predominantly white society. After first observing that children tend to acquire most of the psychological and social characteristics of the families and communities in which they are reared, he adds:

> It is therefore possible that black children reared in white families and communities will develop antiblack psychological and social characteristics.[27]

Chimuzie's remarks suggest a prior conclusion not drawn from the limited statistics available. He assumes too much license in postulating what might be true had the necessary information been available: "Black children reared in white families and communities will develop antiblack psychological and social characteristics." Even if children do adopt most of the psychological and social characteristics of their families and communities, who is to say those characteristics will necesarily conflict with their own racial identity? On the contrary, available data on transracially adopted children between ages three and eight suggest the opposite. These children have not developed self-hate with regard to their racial identity or awareness.

It is equally significant that white, adoptive siblings in these cases have not exhibited antiblack attitudes or pro-white racial preferences. From the available data, transracial adoption appears to benefit both the transracially adopted children themselves and their white, adoptive siblings. This can only serve as a positive harbinger.

In 1974 Grow and Shapiro stated that at least 66-75 percent of the transracially adopted children they studied did not have negative attitudes toward their own race. They felt that this demonstrated that transracial adoption is not a vehicle of cultural genocide as suggested by its opponents. They stated,

> Given the racist elements in American society, it seems unlikely that any group of black children, adopted or otherwise, would have shown a significantly lower degree of negative feelings about blackness. . . .[28]

Grow and Shapiro end their rebuttal to Chimuzie by placing the arguments against transracial adoption into the perspective of personal biases:

Those who have come to the conclusion that transracial adoption is wrong usually hold convictions as strong as Chimuzie. One is hard put to imagine any feasible research project that would change this position. . . . Is there really a debate?[29]

Organizations Opposed to Transracial Adoption

The two organizations opposed to transracial adoption are the National Association of Black Social Workers (NABSW) and its New York chapter, which sponsors the Child Adoption and Counseling Referral Program. The membership in these organizations is composed almost exclusively of social workers employed in a wide variety of settings. Child welfare represents only one such setting.

In the past, the NABSW has voiced strong opposition to transracial adoption:

> We know there are numerous alternatives to the placement of Black children with white families. . . . Black families can be found when agencies alter their requirements, methods of approach. . . . We denounce the assertion that blacks will not adopt. . . . We stand firmly in the conviction that a white home is not a suitable placement for Black children and contend it is totally unnecessary.[30]

Since then, NABSW rhetoric, but not its opposition to the practice, has become somewhat muted. There are now fewer references to transracial adoption as a "lethal incursion on the black family" or a conspiracy by whites to rob blacks of their children.[31] In a letter to *Opportunity,* the president of the NABSW said,

> NABSW feels that it must reaffirm its stand against transracial adoption. Although we strongly agree that a permanent home for a child is preferable to life in foster care. . . , it does not seem that transracial adoptions are a necessary or viable alternative. . . , as there are many black families willing and able to adopt.[32]

Joyce Ladner, a black sociologist, discussed the NABSW in an article that appeared in *Ebony:*

> They're [NABSW] still unalterably opposed to transracial adoption. . . . But I don't think you'll find anyone who will agree it's better for a black child to remain in an institution rather than in a white home. . . . I just can't believe that [an institution] is better than a white home.[33]

In 1978 the New York chapter of the NABSW formally revised the national organization's 1972 statement on transracial adoption. The statement reaffirms the position taken in the letter to *Opportunity* and reflects Ladner's belief (and the preceding NABSW statement) that transracial adoption is preferable to life in an institution or foster home:

> The position paper on transracial adoption *never* stated such a policy nor do we advocate such a policy.[34]

But the letter restated the NABSW's opposition to transracial adoption and added that this type of adoption is anachronistic.

> Black adoptive homes can be found for black children—thereby negating the need for transracial adoption. . . . (There is) . . . overwhelming evidence from black adoptive projects across the nation that black homes can be found for the so-called "hard to place," as well as easy to place black child. . . . It should be emphasized that the options for children trapped in the Child Welfare System are not solely between a white adoptive home or a life or institutionalization. There are black families willing and able to adopt. . . .[35]

The NABSW appears to be devoting less energy to lashing out at perceived white arrogance and more energy to changing the circumstances that make transracial adoption a viable alternative, that is, increasing the number of qualified black adoptors. The NABSW has shifted from rhetoric to programming geared toward locating black adoptive families.

Black-Adoption-Related Organizations

Black-sponsored programs to attract adoptive black families are quite successful. The New York chapter's Child Adoption Counseling and Referral service is an example. Begun in 1978, the service has three functions:

To recruit black adoptive families

To educate the black community

To work to change child agency policies and state laws that make it difficult for blacks to adopt[36]

The service is not a child-placement agency. Rather, it actively recruits potential black adoptive families. Volunteer black social workers conduct interviews and screen prospective adopters *prior to* referring them to adoption agencies. In effect, social workers are reducing the traditionally high black disqualification rate by alleviating commonly held black fears and suspicions of large (racist) organizations. Role playing is used with the families, covering the types of questions they are likely to be asked by adoption-agency caseworkers. Once a prospective black family becomes skilled in the worker-applicant interaction, they are referred to an appropriate child-welfare agency.

The program has met with considerable success. Between 1975 and 1978, they received 3,000 inquiries, interviewed 400 prospective adopters, and referred 285 to child-welfare agencies. As of 1978, 75 children were placed with black families. As impressive as this figure is, the service contends that it could have been greater if the agencies had had more efficient procedures for releasing children and greater willingness to view black families as potential adopters.

Potential adopters are drawn from a wide area around New York City, but similar programs have been initiated in other states. The Association of Black Social Workers' Adoption Recruitment and Referral Service has been established in New Jersey; Advocates for Black Adoption Association of Black Social Workers in Dallas, Texas; and Open Arms Adoption Service Association of Black Social Workers in San Francisco. Additional service-type operations are scheduled to begin in Los Angeles and Baltimore.

These programs do not place children on their own but serve instead as socializing and referral agencies. Some black child-welfare agencies, however, combine all three phases of the adoption process: recruitment, evaluation, and placement. These include the Afro-American Family and Community Services, Inc., in Chicago; Homes for Black Children in Detroit; and the Women's Christian Alliance in Philadelphia.

In addition, there are black-operated arms of larger (white) parent agencies: Harlem-Dowling in New York City; Tayari in San Diego; and the Nassau County Operation Placement in Nassau County, New York. Several white-inspired programs within larger agencies also are devoted to the recruitment of nonwhite families for nonwhite children. The Children's Advocate, located in Illinois, and the Delaware Valley Adoption Agency (DVAC) of Maryland, Delaware, and New Jersey represent such efforts.

The DVAC has had particular success. In seven years (1972-1979), this organization has located homes for more than 650 hard-to-place children. Black children represented a significant percentage. Using the black media and black adoptive parents as recruiters, DVAC is currently developing a large-scale black adoptive parent recruitment program covering the three states involved. DVAC's director recently commented:

> We know that Black families had traditionally cared for children within their community when their own parents were not able to. We knew, however, we had to develop techniques and methods for providing these families with information about many other children waiting for homes as well.[37]

These sentiments appear in almost every discussion of recruitment of black adoptive parents. It is quite possible that the children currently being informally cared for outnumber the approximately 100,000 black children now identified as adoptable. If these figures were known, it is estimated that the proportion of black adoptions would far exceed white adoptions.

Tayari (Swahili for "family and tribul unity") was established in 1971. It is another example of successful black recruitment of black adopters.[38] An organizational arm of the San Diego County Department of Public Welfare, Tayari is located in the heart of San Diego's black community. In 1971, 387 children, including 96 blacks, were placed in adoptive homes by the department. The black children were adopted by two-parent families in which at least one parent was black. Although the department's policies included transracial adoption, 25 black children were not adopted. Eschewing traditional approaches to adoption (middle-class social workers attempting to locate middle-class adoptive parents), Tayari employs black-community workers to operate in the streets,

> returning them [the workers] to a method of practice that existed before the professional social worker was seduced by the psychiatric medical model.[39]

Tayari provides services that are essentially community based or black oriented. Tayari responds to telephone calls from prospective adopters not with a packet of forms but by sending a worker to the caller's home. Forms are not introduced until a relationship is established between client and worker. Where potential adopters cannot be seen in an office, park benches and automobiles are substituted as meeting places. Traditional business hours are also abandoned in order to meet the convenience of prospective adopters.

Black organizations such as the NAACP help recruit staff members involved in religious, cultural, and political activities within the black community. However, effective outreach is not possible without county administrative support. Financial and moral support from the established agency was one of the most important factors in recruiting nonwhite adopters.

With the help of the county, Tayari began a publicity campaign to recruit black adopters from the black community. Speakers were sent to colleges, inservice training programs were conducted with other agencies, and columns and articles appeared in the black press:

> Posters, brochures, radio and T.V. spot announcements were used. Personal appearances were made at service clubs, PTA events, businessman's breakfasts and ghetto festivals. Presentations were adapted to the particular needs of each group.[40]

One of the most important sources of potential adoptive families, however, still appeared to be informal referrals.

Tayari's success was not measured only by the number of children placed inracially or by the number of potential adoptive families on a waiting list. It was measured in increased black awareness of the large numbers of parentless black children spending their early years in institutions or foster care.

It should be kept in mind that no responsible individual or group ever advocated transracial adoption over inracial adoption. Transracial adoption came about only because of the failure of the foster-care system to provide stable, long-term placements for parentless children. Foster care was intended to place children with temporary families pending the development of permanent placements. However, over time the foster-care system was left to provide both the initial and final placements. Many children tended to get lost or drift in the system because of its inability to deal with them on a long-term basis.

There is a certain distasteful logic to the argument that children remain in foster care because child-care agencies have no financial incentive to do otherwise. Most adoption agencies receive payments only for the provision of services related to foster care. The longer a child is kept in foster care, the longer the sponsoring agency is reimbursed for that care. This generally does not hold for adoption. Once a child is removed from the foster-care rolls by adoption, the agency can no longer count him or her for purposes of reimbursement. In other words, it literally does not pay for a child-welfare agency to support large-scale adoption programs. In 1977 it was found that about one third of the children in foster care in New York City remained in that system 5.5 years longer than necessary. The city comptroller's office stated:

> What exists is a fiscal incentive structure that pays agencies for keeping children in foster care, but does not reward them for discharging children . . . into permanent homes. . . .[41]

It is currently estimated that there are approximately 500,000-750,000 children in out-of-home placements across the country.[42] Over 50 percent of these are foster placements. Other types of placements include agency and proprietary group homes, boarding homes, residential treatment facilities, and child-welfare institutions.[43] Over one-third (39 percent) of the children in out-of-home placements are nonwhite.[44] Estimates show that 100,000 children in out-of-home placements are eligible for adoption, of whom about 40,000 are nonwhite. Foster-care systems seem unable to move adoptable, nonwhite children into permanent placements. This lack of direction in the foster-care system is probably one of the most important contributors to the development of transracial adoption.

Because large numbers of adoptable nonwhite children are available within the foster-care system, white couples seeking to adopt are tempted to view them as easy marks. Prospective white adoptive parents seem less inclined to adopt special-needs children so foster children appear more attractive. These white families will probably continue to exert pressure on child-care agencies.

Native-American Opposition

The case of Native Americans is a special one. Native Americans have been subjected to a singularly tragic fate, and their children have been particularly vulnerable.

Native Americans have traditionally practiced an informal "open adoption" with the extended family. The paternal uncle held first option, but if he was unable or unwilling to adopt the child, the biological parent(s) chose another adoptive family within the tribe. The adopters assumed full responsibility for the child, but the biological parent(s) retained visitation rights and maintained close contact with the adoptive family and the child.

Nevertheless, vast numbers of Native-American children have been adopted transracially and, to a very real extent, robbed of their cultural heritage.[45] As recently as 1974, up to 35 percent of all Native-American children were removed from their families and placed in foster care, institutionalized, or adopted. In 1972, one out of four Native-American children under one year of age was adopted in Minnesota. These children were being placed into foster care at a rate approximately five times greater than that for non-Native Americans. By 1978 Minnesota reported that 90 percent of all nonrelated Native-American adoptions were transracial. In 1968 Native-American minors constituted 7 percent of the population and 70 percent of all adoptions in South Dakota. In Wisconsin, the likelihood of Native-American children being removed from their families is 1,600 percent greater than that for non-Native Americans. In Washington State, Native Americans constitute less than 2 percent of the population, but 19 percent of the adoptions. Only 19 of 119 Native-American children were adopted by Native-American families. The remaining 100 were adopted transracially. In 1969 a sixteen-state report indicated that about 85 percent of all Native-American children in foster care were placed transracially.

In 1978 Shyne and Schroeder found that Native-American children constituted 2 percent of all children legally free for adoption in the United States, or approximately 2,040 children.[46] Overall, the rate at which Native-American children are being adopted is 20 times higher than the national rate.[47]

The Indian Child Welfare Act of 1978 (PL95-608) was designed to prevent the decimation of Indian tribes and the breakdown of Indian families by transracial placement of Native-American children.[48]

Sect. 2

There is no resource that is more vital to the continued existence and integrity of Indian tribes than their children and that the United States has a direct interest, as trustee, in protecting Indian children who are members of or are eligible for membership in an Indian tribe;

(4) that an alarmingly high percentage of Indian families are broken up by the removal, often unwarranted, of their children from them by nontribal public and private agencies and that an alarmingly high percentage of such children are placed in non-Indian foster and adoptive homes and institutions; and

(5) that the States, exercising their recognized jurisdiction over Indian child custody proceedings through administrative and judicial bodies, have often failed to recognize the essential tribal relations of Indian people and the cultural and social standards prevailing in Indian communities and families.

Sect. 3

The Congress hereby declares that it is the policy of this Nation to protect the best interests of Indian children and to promote the stability and security of Indian tribes and families by the establishment of minimum Federal standards for the removal of Indian children from their families and the placement of such children in foster or adoptive homes which will reflect the unique values of Indian culture, and by providing for assistance to Indian tribes in the operation of child and family service programs.

Reduction of transracial placements is supported in Title 1, in which all proceedings dealing with Native-American child custody are transferred to tribal jurisdiction:

Title I: Child Custody Proceedings

Sec. 101 (a) An Indian tribe shall have jurisdiction exclusive as to any State over any child custody proceedings involving an Indian child who resides or is domiciled within the reservation of such tribe. . . . Where an Indian child is a ward of a tribal court, the Indian tribe shall retain exclusive jurisdiction, notwithstanding the residence or domicile of the child.

(b) In any State court proceeding for the foster care placement of, or termination of parental rights to, an Indian child not domiciled or residing within the reservation of the Indian child's tribe, the court, in the absence of good cause to the contrary, shall transfer such proceeding to the jurisdiction of the tribe. . . .

The most important provision of this act for transracial adoption appears in Title I:

Sec. 105 (a) In any adoptive placement of an Indian child under State law, a preference shall be given, in the absence of good cause to the contrary, to a placement with a (1) member of the child's extended family; (2) other members of the Indian child's tribe; or (3) other Indian families.

(b) In any foster care preadoptive placement, a preference shall be given, in the absence of good cause to the contrary, to a placement with

(i) a member of the Indian child's extended family;

(ii) a foster home licensed, approved, or specified by the Indian child's tribe;

(iii) an Indian foster home licensed or approved by an authorized non-Indian licensing authority; or

(iv) an institution for children approved by an Indian tribe or operated by an Indian organization which has a program suitable to meet the Indian child's needs.

The law makes it almost impossible for non-Native-American couples to adopt or receive Native-American children in foster placement. PL95-608 is intended to safeguard Native-American culture by keeping families and tribes together and within their native environments.

Title II: Indian Child and Family Programs

Sec. 201 (a) The Secretary is authorized to make grants to Indian tribes and organizations in the establishment and operation of Indian child and family service programs on or near reservations and in the preparation and implementation of child welfare codes. The objective of every Indian child and family service program shall be to prevent the breakup of Indian families and, in particular, to insure that the permanent removal of an Indian child from the custody of his parent or Indian custodian shall be a last resort.

PL95-608 resulted from almost 10 years' effort by individuals and organizations sensitive to the needs of Native-American peoples. It makes tribes, states, and federal governmental agencies responsible for its implementation. The Indian Child Welfare Act will be of little value, however, if foster placements and adoptive parents from Native-American cultures are not recruited in sufficient numbers to absorb the children available for placement.

With the notable exception of the Navaho and Chippewa, many tribes have maintained inadequate records so that it is quite difficult to establish a child's tribal identity. Record-keeping procedures must be improved. In addition, tribes will need trained child-care workers, expanded court systems, and social services for families and children. Nonwhite (especially black) child-welfare models can and probably will serve as general guides with respect to advocacy, recruitment of foster and adoptive placements, and general organization in reducing transracial placement. No doubt, Native Americans will learn rapidly from the experiences of other nonwhite groups.

Arguments and Groups in Favor of Transracial Adoption

The majority of organizations supporting transracial adoption are child welfare oriented. Their activities are aimed at securing a permanent home for every parentless child, although transracial adoption is not a specific mission. Their goal is to achieve permanence for children who need families. If this can best be accomplished through transracial placement, then that will be the plan of choice. Their focus differs from the anti-transracial organizations, which are concerned primarily with the placement of nonwhite children through means other than transracial adoption.

Foremost among the organizations favoring transracial adoption as a viable option is the North American Council on Adoptable Children (NACAC). NACAC includes 400 local chapters throughout the United States and Canada and represents a broad coalition of individuals and adoptive parent groups. Their goal is to have every adoptable child adopted.

At a recent hearing in conjunction with the 1980 White House conference on Families, NACAC's president testified:

> We believe every child has the right to a loving, "forever" family of his or her own. For a great many children now in foster or institutional care, permanency and love can *only* be found through adoption. . . .
>
> We are not talking here about the adoption of racially-matched infants by white, middle-class couples. *That is not adoption today* (authors' emphasis). . . . "Adoptable children" today include many who are older, who are of school age, who are emotionally troubled, physically handicapped, of mixed or minority race, or members of sibling groups. These are "special needs" adoptable children. They need special families. . . . We know such families exist. . . .
>
> However, built into the very system that exists to serve children, there are specific barriers which make permanence difficult or impossible for great numbers of children. . . .
>
> Criteria and methods for recruiting and approving applicants . . . eliminate the very people most able to meet the needs of waiting children. . . .[49]

Most individuals and groups who support transracial adoption belong to NACAC.[50] It acts as an advocacy group for children and families, providing information and public education on adoption (for example, intercountry, transracial, subsidized, single parent). Through its quarterly magazine, *Adoptalk,* and its annual conference, NACAC presents a wide range of topics, "legislative alerts," and human-interest issues representing the spectrum of adoption concerns. It was quite influencial in lobbying for the 1978 passage of the Opportunities for Adoption Act (PL95-266), for which Congress appropriated $5 million. Among its provisions, the bill calls for a National Adoption Information Exchange, a model adoption law, a study of unlicensed adoption homes, and education and training programs.

With passage of the Opportunities for Adoption Act, NACAC received a three-year grant designed to speed placement of hard-to-place adoptable children. The project focuses on three crucial national programs: (1) adoption advocacy to help in the organization of new adoptive groups; (2) adoption education and family recruitment with a specific minority-group program; and (3) a training program for adoption-agency personnel.[51]

This grant (a total of $600,000) will greatly expand the influence of NACAC in the adoption field. Each of the three mandated nationwide programs will have an important impact on transracial adoption. Those programs geared toward prospective nonwhite adoptive parents may, in fact, verify the view of many nonwhite people: that when enough money and energy are devoted to the recruitment of nonwhite adoptive families, adoptable children's needs will be met.

The Council on Adoptable Children (COAC) also favors transracial adoption as a means to achieve permanence for children. It was founded in Michigan in the late 1950s by a biologically fecund family who, after four years and 22 rejections, finally adopted a hard-to-place child. COAC was established when they joined with other adoptive families to find prospects for available children. Most local chapters of COAC are members of NACAC.

NACAC and COAC operate essentially independently. This is not the case with other influencial groups who support transracial adoption. Most exist as programs or subunits within the Child Welfare League of America, the organization responsible for Standards for Adoption Services.

The North American Center on Adoption (NACA) and its activity arm, the Adoption Resource Exchange of North America (ARENA), are among the league's most forceful and successful programs for hard-to-place children.

NACA focuses on the special-needs group among those children legally eligible for adoption. They are defined by age, race, and/or physical or emotional handicap. NACA publishes *Adoption Report,* a quarterly fact sheet, sponsors nationwide programs describing the needs of these children, and supports programs that encourage their adoption. In addition, it offers child-welfare agencies specialized training and consultation services in all matters of child welfare. NACA, like NACAC, is a legislative advocate for children. Together, they were instrumental in passage of the Child Abuse Prevention and Treatment and Adoption Reform Act of 1978.

ARENA, established in 1967, is the operational arm of NACA. It functions as a clearinghouse, giving assistance to adoption agencies nationwide in recruiting prospective adoptive parents for hard-to-place children registered with ARENA. By 1976, 1,750 children were placed.[52] ARENA views transracial adoption as an option for some nonwhite children, but its main concern is the child's best interest. ARENA does not favor any one type of placement over another. Like all other child-welfare organizations, ARENA recognizes the desirability of intracial adoption.

ARENA's Black Outreach Program is typical of its efforts to achieve inracial permanent placements for black children. It was established in early 1978 to locate black adoptive families for black children registered with ARENA. Their methods include educational programs in black communities and self-awareness sessions about black people. Several years before the Black Outreach Progam began, ARENA had established a program in cooperation with the Bureau of Indian Affairs to locate Indian homes for adoptable Indian children.

The Indian and Black Outreach Programs indicate ARENA's thrust: inracial placement is preferred, but transracial placement is not ruled out as an alternative. Like most other organizations with favorable attitudes toward transracial adoption, ARENA is not an adoption agency itself.

In addition to these four organizations, there are literally scores of citizen groups throughout the United States and Canada that support transracial adoption. Groups such as Friends of All Children, Adopt A Child Today (ACT), Open Door Society, Room for One More, Adoptive Parent Association, Children's Home Society of California, Families Adopting Children Everywhere (FACE), Interracial Family Association, and Plan Loving Adoptions Now (PLAN) all favor transracial adoption.

These diverse organizations all had similar beginnings. Groups of concerned families banded together with the common purpose of achieving permanent homes for children in need. Families provide each other with emotional support through meetings and the social networks these meetings create. The groups offer family-centered activities (for example, picnics), where adopted children are given opportunities to meet each other. These are particularly valuable for transracially adopted children. Many of these citizen groups now advocate more humane social legislation in the field of child welfare, sponsor community-education programs, and play an active role in recruiting prospective adoptive parents.

While opponents of transracial adoption have a forum to express their opposition (for example, NABSW), transracial adoption supporters have no such central voice. The ability of these groups to influence child-welfare decision-makers is further limited by two important factors: (1) They lack any substantial financial backing; and (2) they are not considered a political constituency, as are some of the more vocal anti-transracial-adoption groups, whose membership is almost exclusively nonwhite.

The Interracial Family Association (IFA) of Seattle, Washington, is concerned with unifying the policies of pro-transracial-adoption forces. IFA formed a task force on transracial adoption that recognized that "transracial adoption has been a controversial subject. From white racists to black separatists, it has been besieged by opposition. . . ."[53] The IFA

Task Force issued "Guidelines for Transracial Adoption Participants [parents and agencies]." The guidelines assert that transracial adoption should be defined as a first choice in many cases rather than strictly as an alternative.

> The family must be seen as the most viable choice for the child; transracial adoption may be valid even when a family of like race is available. We refuse to be defined in a second class way both for ourselves and for the developing self-esteem of our children.[54]

Concluding Remarks

In condemning transracial adoption, nonwhite groups have actually increased white awareness. Nonwhite adoptive families *do* exist and could be located if traditional agency practices and policies were modified. Adoption agencies probably do exclude prospective nonwhite adoptive families systematically, whether consciously or otherwise.

In its 1978 statement, the New York chapter of the NABSW noted renewed white pressure on adoption agencies to increase transracial adoption.[55] The exact nature of the pressure was not described, but the NABSW cited an 11-percent increase in transracial adoption since 1978.[56] The statement goes on to say that even if the NABSW were to support transracial adoption, the majority of children currently in foster care would not be affected.

> Only one percent or less of the white families willing to adopt Black children request children who are most in need of families: children over eight (8) years of age; sibling groups, and emotionally and physically handicapped children.[57]

Since white adoptive parents seem to shun older children of any race with physical handicaps, they turn to the healthy, black infants for whom black parents are available.

The service's media efforts, however, have found changes in child preferences among prospective black adopters. Black couples requesting children between the ages of seven and fourteen rose from 32 percent in 1975 to 46 percent in 1977. Black families specifically requesting infants dropped from 20 percent in 1978 to 17 percent in 1977. The service concluded that "for Black prospective adoptive families, infants are *not* the most desirable age."[58]

These figures imply that transracial adoption is not viable in reducing the population of black children most in need of adoptive families. Rather, black recruitment of black families offers the greater opportunity for thinning the ranks of black school-age children in foster care.[59]

Even though most nonwhite (especially black) social workers remain opposed to transracial adoption, the social-work profession and most prospective white adopters remain ambivalent. A 1975 study of adoption workers nationwide showed that 86 percent would support the adoption application of a racially mixed couple, and 55 percent would accept the adoption application of a white couple who wanted to adopt a biracial child.[60]

In 1977 Arnold R. Silverman and William Feigelman surveyed adoptive parents across the country to profile white adopters of nonwhite children.[61] The study emphasized nonwhite adoptions, primarily intercountry adoptions from Asia. Questionnaire responses measured nontraditional, transitional, and traditional family life by "divergence from traditional roles" (for example, father's participation in child-care activities such as diapering, feeding, and playing; and attitudes toward wife's employment and ability to be a good mother). The authors found a significant relationship between a father's participation in child-rearing activities (nontraditional) and a (white) family's willingness to adopt black children. Only 20 percent of traditionally defined families indicated that they would adopt a black child.

The study also identified a strong relationship between a family's support for maternal employment while mothering and the family's willingness to adopt a black child. In fact, 19 percent of the families who expressed approval had already adopted a black child, whereas only 4 percent of the families who strongly disapproved had done so.

The Silverman and Feigelman data suggest that recruitment efforts should be targeted specifically to those groups most willing to adopt nonwhite children and to those families who have already done so. Adoption subsidies for most (if not all) available black children (as suggested by the Model Adoption Act in appendix B), should make them extremely desirable. The Silverman-Feigelman survey augments our own findings in support of transracial adoption. There *are* white parents willing to adopt nonwhite children, and there *are* nonwhite children needing adoptive homes.

Notes

1. Chester Sheard, *Muhammad Speaks*, 14 August 1973, p. 11.
2. *New York Times*, 8 April 1972; National Association of Black Social Workers Conference, Nashville, Tennessee, 4-9 April 1972; "Should Whites Adopt Black Children?" *Encore* (January 1973):18.
3. Eugene D. Genovese, *Roll, Jordan, Roll: The World the Slaves Made* (Pantheon, New York, 1974); Kenneth B. Clark, *Dark Ghetto* (Harper and Row, New York, 1965); E. Franklin Frazier, *The Negro Family in the United States*, rev. ed. (MacMillan, New York, 1957); Gunnar Myrdal, *The American Dilemma*, rev. ed. (Harper and Row, New York, 1962).

4. Leon Chestang, "The Dilemma of Bi-racial Adoption," *Social Work* (May 1972):100; Amuzie Chimuzie, "Transracial Adoption of Black Children," *Social Work* (July 1975):296; *Opportunity*, A Division of the Boys and Girls Aid Society of Oregon, 2301 Glisan Street, Portland, OR 97210. Letter from the National Association of Black Social Workers, Portland, Oregon, 11 August 1977.

5. The Department of Health, Education and Welfare discontinued producing nationwide adoption figures. These figures were taken from a paper prepared for the Model Adoption Legislation and Procedures Advisory Panel and quoted in *Adoption Report* 4 (No. 3) (Summer 1979). These figures were later corroborated in a study by Ann W. Shyne and Anita G. Schroeder, *National Study of Social Services to Children and Their Families: An Overview*, The National Center for Child Advocacy, U.S. Department of Health, Education and Welfare, Office of Human Development Services, Administration for Children, Youth and Families, Children's Bureau, DHEW Publications #(OHDS) 78-30150, Washington, D.C., 1978.

Varying figures have been produced for specific regions in the country. For example, COAC reports that blacks and Hispanics account for 60 and 30 percent, respectively, of the 22,000 children in New York City's foster-care system. Proportionally about 3,000 are available for adoption. [*Adoptalk* (National Council of Adoptive Organizations, Minneapolis, Minnesota) 5 (No. 2) (February-March 1980)]. Even for these children, there are not enough adoptive parents.

6. *NASW News* (National Association of Social Workers, New York) 22 (No. 3) (March 1977):17-19.

7. Ibid., p. 30.

8. *NASW News* 24 (No. 7) (July 1979):17, 20.

9. *NASW News* 25 (No. 1) (January 1980):17-31.

10. Ibid., p. 20.

11. Ibid., p. 3.

12. Martin Waldron, "Lesbian Foster Parents Used in New Jersey," *New York Times*, 27 November 1979, p. 32.

13. Ibid.

14. Child Welfare League of America, *Standards for Adoption Service*, revised (Child Welfare League of America, New York, 1978), p. ix.

15. See Rita Simon and Howard Altstein, *Transracial Adoption* (Wiley Interscience, New York, 1977), pp. 47-48, for an overview of the league's position statements on transracial adoption from 1958 to 1973.

16. Child Welfare League of America, *Standards*, footnote 14, p. xi.

17. Ibid., section 1.1, p. 11.

18. Ibid., section 1.2, p. 12.

19. Ibid., section 0.8, p. 7.

20. Ibid., section 4.2, pp. 43-44.

21. Ibid., section 4.5, pp. 44-45.

22. *Transracial Adoption Update: 1978*, New York Chapter National Association of Black Social Workers, mimeograph, pp. 4-5.

23. Chimuzie, "Transracial Adoption of Black Children," *Social Work* (July 1975):296-301.

24. Elizabeth Herzog, Cecelia E. Sudia, and Jane Harwood, "Some Opinions on Finding Families for Black Children," *Children* (July-August 1971):147.

25. Alicia Howard, David D. Royce, and John A. Skerl, "Transracial Adoption: The Black Community Perspective," *Social Work* 22 (No. 3) (May 1977):184-189.

26. Ibid., pp. 185-186.

27. Amuzie Chimuzie, "Bold but Irrelevant: Grow and Shapiro on Transracial Adoption," *Child Welfare* 56 (No. 2) (February 1977):75-86. A critique of Grow and Shapiro's study.

28. Lucille J. Grow and Deborah Shapiro, *Black Children—White Parents: A Study of Transracial Adoption* (Child Welfare League of America, New York, 1974), p. 88.

29. Ibid., p. 91.

30. Edmond D. Jones, "On Transracial Adoption of Black Children," *Child Welfare* 51 (No. 3) (March 1972):38.

31. Ibid.

32. President of the National Association of Black Social Workers, letter to *Opportunity*, 11 August 1977, p. 6.

33. Michele Burgen, "Should Whites Adopt Black Children?" *Ebony* (December 1977):68.

34. *Transracial Adoption Update:1978*, p. 1.

35. Ibid., pp. 1-2.

36. Ibid., p. 6.

37. *Adoptalk* (National Council of Adoptive Organizations) 4 (No. 3) (November 1979):5.

38. Jacqueline Nielson, "Tayari: Black Homes for Black Children," *Child Welfare* 55 (No. 1) (January 1976):41.

39. Ibid., p. 43.

40. Ibid., p. 45.

41. *New York Times*, 2 June 1977.

42. These figures are estimates. Knitzer reported [Jane Knitzer, *Children Without Homes* (Children's Defense Fund, Washington, D.C., 1978), pp. 1-2] that child-welfare officials nationwide were unable to determine the length of time spent in foster care for 53 percent of their children and did not know the ages and races of 49 percent and 54 percent, respectively [*Adoptalk* 5 (No. 2) (February-March 1980):1].

43. We must emphasize that there is no reliable data on children in out-of-home placement, especially foster care. As Knitzer states, "Counties know *where* to send payments, although they may not know for *whom* they are sending them." (Knitzer, *Children Without Homes*, p. 187.)

44. Shyne and Schroeder, *National Study of Social Services to Children*, p. 132.

45. David Fanshel, *Far from the Reservation: The Transracial Adoption of American Indian Children* (Scarecrow Press, Metuchen, New Jersey, 1972). This remains one of the best portraits of transracial adoption among Native American children.

46. Shyne and Schroeder, *National Study of Social Services to Children*.

47. "An Indian Perspective on Adoption," Workshop at the Sixth North American Conference on Adoptable Children, Seattle, Washington, 27–29 July 1978.

48. For an excellent discussion of historic and legal events leading to enactment of PL 95–608, see "A Report Together with Dissenting Views," Report #1386, House of Representatives, Committee on Interior and Insular Affairs, Washington, D.C., 1979. (Morris Udall, Chairman)

49. *Adoptalk* 5 (No. 2) (February–March 1980):6.

50. Recently, however, the director of New York's COAC stated that transracial adoption is a "painful subject." Arguing that adoptable children should be kept within their own cultures, she stated that minority adoptive parents can offer nonwhite children what whites cannot: an identity. Although she felt that race should not be a variable in a placement decision, reality dictates otherwise. *Adoptalk* 5 (No. 2) (February–March 1980).

51. *Adoptalk* 4 (No. 3) (November 1979).

52. *ARENA News*, Newsletter of the Adoptive Resource Exchange of North America, Annual Report (Child Welfare League of America, New York, 1976).

53. *Adoptalk* 4 (No. 1) (First Quarter 1979):12.

54. Ibid.

55. *Transracial Adoption Update: 1978*.

56. Ibid. On 29 September 1979, one of the authors of this work contacted E. Goddard, director of the Boys and Girls Aid Society of Oregon. This organization publishes *Opportunity*, a fact sheet devoted to transracial adoption issues. It compiles and publishes figures on the numbers of nonwhite children adopted by whites. *Opportunity* is, to the best knowledge of the author and the society's director, the only publication of its nature. Goddard stated that, since 1975, his organization no longer compiled such information and, "no other organization has data." He stated that he had no additional figures on transracial adoption since 1975. According to *Opportunity* published in 1976, 831 nonwhite children were transracially adopted in 1975 ("National Survey of black children adopted in 1975"). *Opportunity* has not

published any figures since then, although preliminary figures for 1976 indicate that 1,070 black children were transracially adopted. Day cites *Opportunity* as her source [Dawn Day, *The Adoption of Black Children* (Lexington, Mass.; Lexington Books, D.C. Heath and Company, 1979), p. 93, table 6-1].

The Boys and Girls Society is not alone in discontinuing collection of data relating to transracial adoption. At the federal level, the National Center for Social Statistics was abolished in 1977. The government no longer compiles national adoption figures and will not do so until the Cranston Bill takes effect in 1980–1981. Elaine Schwartz of the Children's Bureau said to this author on 6 June 1979 that the 1981 figures probably would not be available until 1985.

In 1975, the last year for which national adoption figures are available, only 42 states reported, and 9 of them submitted either incomplete or unuseable data.

Jones and Else stated [Edmond D. Jones and John F. Else, "Racial and Cultural Issues in Adoption," *Child Welfare* 58 (9 June 1979):373–382] that about 25 percent of all black adoptions in 1976 were transracial. As their source, the authors cited a 1976 telephone interview with Stuart R. Stimmel, Goddard's predecessor at the society. Neither Goddard nor his assistant could confirm this figure.

57. *Transracial Adoption Update:1978*, p. 3. The Public Information Director of New York State's Council on Voluntary Child Care Agencies reports that 50 percent of the children in that state's foster-care system enter at age twelve or older. There are 48,000 children in foster care in New York State (E.J. Dionne, Jr., "Foster Care Once Again is Enveloped in Scandal," *New York Times*, 14 October 1979).

58. *Transracial Adoption Update: 1978*, p. 9.

59. One of the directors of New York City's Council on Adoptable Children recently stated that recruitment must be an ongoing effort. No matter what the child's race, potentially adoptive individuals must continually be sought. Adoption agencies must be convinced that adoptive parents can be located for available children. The public should be informed that children are available for adoption although they (the children) usually will not fit the traditional demographics. If 40 percent of an agency's adoptable children are nonwhite, then an equal amount of time (40 percent) should be devoted to recruiting potentially adoptive nonwhite families. (*Adoptalk* 5 (No. 2) (February–March 1980).

60. Edwin G. Brown and Donald Brieland, "Adoptive Screening: New Data, New Dimensions," *Social Work* 20 (No. 4) (July 1975):291.

61. Arnold R. Silverman and William Feigelman, "Some Factors Affecting the Adoption of Minority Children," *Social Casework* 58 (No. 9) (November 1977):554–558.

5 Court and Legislative Decisions

Since our last review in 1975, the courts have ruled in three important cases involving attempted transracial adoption of nonwhite children by white families. In one case the court ruled in favor of the transracial adoption and in the other two, it ruled that racial differences between the children and the prospective adoptive parents were significant enough to warrant denial of the adoption petitions.[1]

This chapter examines the issues involved in these three cases. It also reviews several recent court rulings with indirect bearing on transracial adoption. Current and pending federal adoption legislation will be considered, even though transracial placement is not specifically at issue because the results of any child-welfare or adoption legislation generally affect transracial adoption as well.

The Courts and Transracial Adoption

In 1978 a New Mexico court (*Jones* v. *State of New Mexico*) ruled against the state Department of Human Resources, which had denied a request from a Mormon couple to adopt their nine-month-old racially mixed, black and white foster son. The boy had been placed with the family when he was four days old. In opposing the adoption, the Department of Human Resources noted that the Church of Jesus Christ of Latter Day Saints (Mormons) barred nonwhites from their priesthood. The trial court judge overruled the department, citing the positive characteristics of the adoptive family. One month prior to this decision, the Mormon church had revoked its long-standing practice of barring nonwhites from the priesthood.[2]

In 1979 a Texas appeals court upheld the ruling of a lower court, awarding permanent custody of a half-Native-American child (Sioux) to her non-Indian grandparents (*Brokenleg* v. *Butts*, No. 78025). In its original ruling, the lower court said it would be "detrimental" and "unnatural" for the child to be returned to her biological mother on a South Dakota Rosebud Sioux reservation. The case attracted considerable attention from advocates of Indian rights.[3]

In 1977 a Georgia county department of family and children's services denied the petition of Mr. and Mrs. Drummond, a white couple, to adopt their three-year-old foster son. The child, who was racially mixed, had been placed for temporary care in the Drummonds's home when he was one month old. Within a year the Drummonds requested permission to adopt him. A federal court of appeals upheld the agency denial because of the racial differences between the foster parents and the child. The court (*Drummond* v. *Fulton County*) contended that in locating the most appropriate adoptive family, legitimate consideration should be given to their respective races. The U.S. Supreme Court later declined to review the decision of the Georgia court. (Justices Brennan and White dissented.) In rendering its decision, the Supreme Court said,

> It is obvious that race did enter into the decision of the Department. It appears to the Court that the consideration of race was properly directed to the best interest of the child and was not an automatic type of thing or of placement, that is, that all blacks go to black families, all whites go to white families, and all mixed children go to black families which would be prohibited.

The Court referred to professional literature on the subject of transracial child placement and claimed that "a couple has no right to adopt a child it is not equipped to rear."[4]

In 1979 a superior court in the state of Connecticut upheld a decision made by the Department of Children and Youth against the petition of white foster parents to adopt the four-month-old black infant placed with them since birth. The court ruled (*Lusa* v. *State of Connecticut*) that it was appropriate for the state to consider the racial backgrounds of the child and the prospective parents in deciding whether to grant the adoption:

> The court has no doubt that the plaintiffs are excellent foster parents. Unfortunately, no family in our present society can be an island. Granted that society and the community should not harbor attitudes against interracial mixture, the subject of the foster-home placement and the adoption is the child, whose life will be affected by the community values and prejudices as they exist, not as they ought to be.[5]

While not denying racial differences as a reason to oppose the adoption, other factors also were noted. One such factor was the state's policy of discouraging foster parents' petitions for children already in their care. The policy was intended to prevent "child shopping." Another consideration was the fact that the foster mother was pregnant with her third child. The prospective parents contended that one of the strongest points against their application in addition to the state's policy toward transracial adoption was that they were of the Bahai faith.[6]

The Connecticut decision reopened the debate about transracial adoption. In a 1979 editorial, the *New York Times* stated:

There is no reason why interracial adoption cannot succeed. Indeed, such adoptions in the past are part of the evidence for the conclusion that race is not the most important factor in human behavior or potential. . . .[7]

The long-term effects of transracial adoption on identity are as yet unknown. Recognizing this, Leona Neal, head of the Child Adoption Counseling and Referral Service of the NABSW's New York chapter wrote in response,

To say that having friends the same race as the child, living in an integrated neighborhood, and having the child attend integrated schools are all that is necessary for a transracial adoption to succeed is to miss entirely, or completely disregard, the importance of ethnic and family identity.[8]

In supporting the court's decision, the American Child Welfare League said,

Black kids will in fact have problems in white homes. In good social work you always ask what is in the best interest of the child, and you try to give him as few problems as possible.[9]

There was also division within the black community itself. White, the director of Connecticut's NAACP, stated, "I don't think it's valid or appropriate to deny adoption on the basis of color."[10] At the same time a black supervisor with the American Child Welfare League, who is responsible for locating black adopters, noted that there are black families waiting for black babies and preschoolers.[11]

The court decisions in two of the three cases are strikes against transracial adoption. Proponents seek to have race disallowed as a legitimate criterion for courtroom consideration.

The emotionalism surrounding transracial adoption, both from supporters and opponents, white and black, is extremely close to the surface. Evidence shows that transracial adoption has ceased almost entirely. Yet when isolated petitions do receive court attention, invariably from prospective white adopters, they are viewed as attempts to wrest black children from their own heritage and culture. The simple argument, "All we (prospective white adopters) wanted to do was love somebody. I don't see anything wrong with that,"[12] is not accepted by nonwhites. They view transracial adoption as a threat to the children's black consciousness. The basic argument against transracial adoption has not changed fundamentally since 1972 when Edmond Jones claimed that whites with the best of intentions cannot produce viable solutions for black problems. He wrote,

The attempt to characterize black people as simply U.S. citizens boiling away in some great cauldron of middle American togetherness is a notion that denies every black citizen of this country his right to be what he is—an Afro-American . . . effectively and distinctly a cultural entity apart.[13]

Court Cases Bearing on Transracial Adoption

The courts are becoming increasingly aware and supportive of nonconventional parenting styles. Several recent decisions reflect this changing attitude. In two cases, courts upheld the rights of homosexuals (both male and female) to adopt and be awarded child custody.

On 21 January 1979 a New York county family court ruled that an ordained minister of the Reformed Church in America, a homosexual, be awarded final custody of a thirteen-year-old boy he had adopted the previous year. In announcing his decision, the judge stated,

> I saw no reason why this adoption should not be permanent. . . . The reverend is providing a good home, the boy loves his adoptive father and wants to be with him. Who knows in this world of ours? You do the best you can and hope it works out.[14]

According to the former executive director of the National Gay Task Force, the courts have allowed several dozen homosexuals to adopt recently.

On 25 July 1979 the New Jersey Court of Appeals overturned a decision by the Appellate Division of Superior Court and ruled that the homosexuality of a parent did not disqualify the parent from being awarded child custody. In its decision, the court said, "[The homosexual mother] had done all that can be expected of a dutiful mother."[15]

These decisions demonstrate continuing faith in the integrity of the family, even though it has taken nontraditional forms.[16] Certainly an adoptive family of a race other than the adopted child's would constitute another nontraditional family form well within the confines of the traditional model that the courts and states have historically supported.

Underlying recent judicial decisions is the fundamental burden of the state to prove a parent(s) unfit and to sanction removal in the child's behalf. In *Delaware* v. *Doe*, the Supreme Court agreed to hear the case of John and Jane Doe, who lost custody of their five children in 1975 when they were declared "unfit." The Court said,

> It is difficult to imagine a statutory standard more vague [offering] no clue to what constitutes unfitness, forcing courts, state officials, and parents to guess at its meaning. . . .[17]

Nevertheless, the Delaware state courts rejected the Doe's contention that the "unfit" label did not meet constitutional specificity. In their petition, the Does asked the Supreme Court to declare that a state must prove its case in a parental termination proceeding by clear and convincing evidence, rather than the lesser standard of the "preponderance of the evidence."[18]

New York and Connecticut have detailed legislation defining the standards for termination of parental rights. Under Connecticut law, a child may be removed from his/her parents only after a finding of abandonment for one year or a finding that the parents have denied the child the necessary care, control, and guidance required for physical and emotional health. New York state law requires a finding that a child's emotional, physical, and mental state was or currently is threatened. The law specifically defines the parental behavior that would constitute the threat.

A Supreme Court ruling in *Delaware* v. *Doe* is likely to have great impact in the field of child welfare. At issue is whether or not the Constitution requires the states to define specific behaviors of unfit parents. If the Court rules that certain unfit behaviors may be applied retroactively, the results would be bureaucratically staggering for the lower courts. More tragic would be the potential psychological consequences for some children and parents.

Such a ruling could enable biological parents to challenge findings of unfitness against them, win a reversal, and then ask a court to void the adoption of his/her child several years after placement. There are precedents for such a situation. After the fall of South Vietnam and Cambodia, for example, many supposedly parentless children were air-lifted to the United States and adopted by American families. When the children's biological parents arrived in the United States, several of these adoptions were challenged and nullified.

In their desire to become parents, some couples take part in foster-care programs. If a child placed in their care becomes legally free for adoption, foster parents have priority over other prospective adoptive parents in most cases.

This situation is illustrated by a recent Maryland case in which a child was placed in foster care by his unwed, teen-aged mother after she was forced out of her alcoholic father's home.[19] The child remained with the same foster family for five years. The biological mother visited occasionally. According to court testimony, a strong relationship developed between the child, his two foster siblings, and his foster parents. At the suggestion of the county social-services department, the foster family began adoption proceedings.

Two years after the child was placed in foster care, the biological mother married and subsequently requested that her child be returned. Her application coincided with the foster parents' adoption petition.

The Maryland Court of Special Appeals ruled that only in extreme cases can a biological mother's claim to her child be denied. The court ordered

the child returned to her. At the time of writing, the case is being appealed
to Maryland's highest court.

The foster and biological mothers summarized the terrible dilemma
created when biological parents attempt to retrieve children who have spent
several years in a foster family:

> In every way, shape, and form, except biologically, David is our son [the
> foster mother said]. We've raised him. . . . Mother's rights or no mother's
> rights, we believe David should have some rights in this, too. . . . If I were
> in Julie's [the biological mother] position, and I really loved him, I think I
> would see that David is part of this family and there is no way I would take
> him away from that.
>
> I've done everything they asked me to do [said the biological mother]. I've
> straightened myself out. I'm more stable. I think about what I'm going to do.
> And now I want David back. . . . He's no stranger. We're talking
> about . . . my son. Nobody ever gets used to the fact that they are not going
> to see their son again. . . . I love my son, and I know he loves me. . . .[20]

Of the seven letters to the editor prompted by this story, all favored leaving the child with his foster family.[21] None supported the court's decision.

Legislative Decisions

The most recently enacted federal legislation (April 1978) that deals with
adoption is PL95-266, "Child Abuse Prevention and Treatment and Adoption Reform Act of 1978." Although this act deals with issues specific to child
abuse, Title II, "Adoption Opportunities," speaks directly to adoption and
has consequences for transracial adoption:

Title II: Adoption Opportunities

Findings and Declaration of Purpose

SC5111. Sec. 201. The Congress hereby finds that many thousands of
children remain in institutions or foster homes solely because of legal and
other barriers to their placement in permanent, adoptive homes; that the majority of such children are of school age, handicapped, or both; that adoption may be the best alternative for assuring the healthy development of such
children; that there are qualified persons seeking to adopt such children who
are unable to do so because of barriers to their placement; and that, in order
both to enhance the stability and love of the child's home environment and to
avoid wasteful expenditures of public funds, such children should not be
maintained in foster care or institutions when adoption is appropriate and
families for them can be found. It is, therefore, the purpose of this title to
facilitate the elimination of barriers to adoption and to provide permanent
and loving home environments for children who would benefit by adoption,
particularly children with special needs. . . .

By passing this act and specifically stating that

> adoption may be the best alternative for assuring the healthy development of [such] children . . . [and therefore] . . . such children should not be maintained in foster care or in institutions when adoption is appropriate and families can be found. . . .

Congress supported what the social-work profession has historically maintained: that a family is the best environment for most children.

Even though the act does not mention it, section 201 has significant implications for transracial adoption. PL95-266 is intended to facilitate adoption for as many children as are legally eligible, especially those facing special barriers. Responsible agencies are mandated to surmount those barriers to find permanent homes whenever adoptive families can be found. Paragraph 2A of section 201 offers child-welfare agencies a mechanism to locate prospective adoptive parents. It specifies that the Department of Health and Human Services shall

> provide for a national adoption and foster care information data gathering and analysis system and a national adoption information exchange system to bring together children who would benefit by adoption and qualified prospective parents who are seeking such children.[22]

The overall intent of Act PL95-266 is clearly to encourage any legitimate action to achieve permanent and loving homes for parentless children.

Section 202 of the act calls for model adoption legislation and procedures to be published in the *Federal Register* not later than 18 months after PL95-266 was enacted (see appendix B).

Section 203 reviews child-welfare legislation with an emphasis on adoption provisions. We assert again that any changes in the field of adoption affect transracial adoption in that it is an inseparable part of adoption policy overall.

History of Federally Sponsored Child-Welfare Funding

Historically the welfare titles of the Social Security Act (SSA) have provided federal monies for two types of aid: (1) cash public assistance and (2) social-service programs or noncash assistance (for example, foster care). Paradoxically, both categories of aid were funded through cash public-assistance programs. Social-service programs were defined as "administrative costs." Several amendments to the SSA were necessary to legitimize the defacto separation of these two categories of aid. Recognition of this division brought on other important developments. Not only was the range of social services increased but, perhaps equally important, these social services could then be offered to individuals who were not receiving public assistance (for example, foster parents). They could be funded through both public and nonpublic agencies, regardless of their status as welfare agencies. This dichotomy called for a 75-percent rate of federal matching funds.

Until 1973 the federal government had no ceiling on the amount of money it could allocate for social services and public assistance (welfare). It provided $3 for every $1 spent by the states. In 1971-1972, an increased number of social-service programs were established by the states. This growth called for a significant increase in federal expenditures. Consequently in 1973 Congress placed a $2.5 billion annual ceiling on federal social-services expenditures. The limit for each state was determined by its population proportional to the entire country. The ceiling was raised to $2.7 billion in 1979.

In 1974 Congress transferred all social-service programs from SSA to Title XX, a newly established services title. It maintained both the 75-percent matching funds and the current $2.5 billion ceiling. However, it added the proviso that no federally funded social services would be delivered to families or individuals whose income exceeded the state's median. Each state's median income was determined annually by DHHS, based on information furnished by the Census Bureau.[23]

By 1979 approximately 5 percent of the monies under Title XX were spent on foster-care services and 11 percent were spent on protective services.[24] On the other hand, Title XX never made any funds available for adoption services. The failure to set aside these funds is evidence that adoption agencies lacked incentive (economic and otherwise) to support or encourage adoption programs. This pertains especially to programs for children perceived as hard to place. The longer children remained in foster care and protective service, the longer adoption agencies received state funding and federal support. This lack of incentive was particularly detrimental for transracial adoption where, for the most part, prospective adoptive parents were available.

Except for the 95th Congress's introduction of HR7200, "Child Welfare Services, Foster Care and Adoption Assistance," the preceding paragraphs illustrate the adoption situation facing the new 97th Congress in 1981. On January 23, almost immediately after Congress convened, Congressman William M. Brodhead (D-Mich.), a co-sponsor of HR7200, introduced HR1291 as an amendment to SSA, Title IV. This amendment called for subsidies for those families willing but unable to adopt for economic reasons. The subsidy was to be provided under the Aid to Families with Dependent Children program (AFDC). On January 25 Congressman George Miller (D-Calif.), also a sponsor of HR7200, introduced HR1523, which, among other child-welfare provisions, spoke directly to the issue of permanent adoption planning for children in foster-care "limbo." Shortly thereafter, the administration introduced its own child-welfare bill (HR3222), "AFDC, Foster Care Subsidy," which expressed strong support for adoption subsidies.

All three bills (HR1291, HR1523, and HR3222) were referred to the House Subcommittee on Public Assistance and Unemployment Compensation of the Ways and Means Committee. The subcommittee formulated a compromise bill (HR3434), "Social Services and Child Welfare Amendments of 1979," which the House passed on 2 August 1979, by a vote of 401 to 2.

HR3434 was then sent to the Senate Committee on Finance, where it was passed 27 September 1979.[25] The committee retained the bill's most important concept, that of federal subsidies to families adopting hard-to-place children but attempted to limit those subsidies to children otherwise eligible for public assistance. This attempt was defeated by an amendment barring any "means test" for parents willing to adopt children eligible for subsidies. Like AFDC children, those adopted under the subsidized-adoption program would be entitled to medicaid regardless of the adoptive parents' financial background.

The Senate Committe on Finance did, however, place a ceiling on subsidy allocations equal to 120 percent of federal monies spent in 1978 on subsidies for foster care and removed the entitlement provision. Deletion of the entitlement provision requires that funds be requested yearly rather than on a continuing basis. Only about 8,000 children now in foster care will be eligible for adoption under this bill if it remains intact after a House-Senate conference.

The most knowledgeable individuals in the child-welfare field believe that the most important provision of any successful adoption legislation is a meaningful subsidy program. They argue that federally supported subsidies are the key to reducing the population of more than 500,000 children in foster-care systems.

Forty-four states (including the District of Columbia) have legislated subsidies for hard-to-place children. Some have yet to design their programs, while others have had subsidized-adoption programs for 10 years. Most recent data indicate that in the last 10 years, the families of approximately 18,000 adopted children are receiving maintenance subsidies or medical assistance. Only one state excludes medical payments from its subsidies.[26]

Comparison of Title IV of the SSA, HR3434, and HR7200

As of 1979 states receive federal monies for child-welfare services through Title IV (B) of the SSA. Although Congress appropriated $266 million for child-welfare services in 1979, only 21 percent ($56.5 million) was actually authorized. However, with state contributions included, about $800 million was spent on child-welfare programs in 1979. Only 3 percent of that total was spent on adoption, as opposed to 73 percent spent for foster care. Twenty-five states reported that no money whatsoever was spent on any type of adoption program. Only one state reported spending no money for foster care.[27]

On 25 October 1979 the Finance Committee's amended version of HR3434 was introduced in the Senate. On October 29, it was passed with 12 additional amendments (seventeen were introduced). One of the rejected amendments would have eliminated federal support for subsidized adoption, severely limiting, if not totally preventing, the potential adoption of hard-to-place children. It was overwhelmingly defeated, 77 to 13.

During the early part of March of 1980, a joint House-Senate conference committee was convened to consider HR3434. Following is a summary of the committee's most important provisions as they relate to our discussion:

1. During fiscal 1980-1981, only $200 million in federal funds will be available for child care, and no state matching funds will be required, even though Title XX has a $2.7 billion ceiling.
2. Title IV-B (Child Welfare Service Program) authorizes $266 million in annual expenditures. In fact, annual appropriations have never exceeded $56.5 million. These appropriations may be used for foster-care payments and other child-welfare services. The newly approved House-Senate version of IV-B prohibits any state from reducing its portion of the $56.5 million below the 1979 level to remain eligible for additional monies under this title.
3. The conference committee ordered that states wishing to receive Title IV-B funds (Aid to Families with Dependent Children—Foster Care) must begin subsidized adoption programs by 1 October 1982.
4. The medicaid definition of "special-needs children" (eligible for SSI, AFDC, or AFDC-Foster Care) will be enforced to determine those subsidized adoptions eligible for federal matching funds.
5. No payment for subsidized adoption may exceed foster-care limitations.
6. Federal matching funds for subsidized adoption shall continue until the child is eighteen years old. Payment shall continue until age twenty-one if the child is mentally or physically handicapped.
7. As of 1 October 1983, individual states will be responsible for subsidies to adoptive families even if they no longer reside in the state.

On 13 June 1980 Congress accepted the House-Senate Conference Report and voted in favor of HR3434. It was signed by the president on

17 June and became known as PL96-262. This concluded efforts begun in 1975 as legislative proposals to improve the foster-care system.

PL96-262 is a major step toward developing a national policy on subsidized adoption. Implementation of federal matching funds for subsidized adoptions should affect adoption agencies' recruitment efforts. The absence of a means test for potential adoptive families is of particular importance: Subsidies will be tied to individual children, and adoptive families will no longer have to maintain residence in the state that originally approved the subsidy in order to remain eligible.

The current push toward a balanced budget (with an expected $15 billion reduction in federal spending) is still a threat to the actual appropriaton of monies allocated for child-welfare services.

Notes

1. *Jones* v. *The State of New Mexico* (Santa Fe District Court), 1978. *Drummond* v. *Fulton County Department of Family and Children's Services* (Georgia) 547 f. 2d, 835 (5th Circuit, 1977); *Lusa* v. *The State of Connecticut*, 2817, 2780. *The Family Law Reporter* J (No. 40) (August 1979):5.

2. "Mormon Couple Wins on Adoption," *New York Times*, 19 June 1978.

3. "Indian Custody," *New York Times*, 19 June 1979.

4. *New York Times*, 29 November 1977.

5. "Court Bars Adoption of a Black by Whites," *New York Times*, 2 August 1979.

6. Dianne Henry, "Whites Find Black-baby Adoptions Harder," *New York Times*, 21 August 1979.

7. "Black Child White Parents," *New York Times*, 6 August 1979.

8. Leona Neal, "No Child Should Be Denied His Heritage," *New York Times*, 8 September 1979.

9. Henry, "Whites Find Black-baby Adoptions Harder."

10. Ibid.

11. Ibid.

12. Ibid.

13. Edmond D. Jones, "Reader's Forum," *Child Welfare* 51 (No. 6) (June 1972):371.

14. George Vecsey, "Approval Given for a Homosexual to Adopt a Boy," *New York Times*, 21 June 1979.

15. "Homosexual Rights on Custody Upheld," *New York Times*, 25 July 1979.

16. For two excellent contrasting discussions of the historic development of the family, see Christopher Lasch, *Haven in a Heartless World:*

The Family Beseiged (New York: Basic Books, 1979); and Jacques Donzelot, *The Policy of Families* (New York: Pantheon, 1980).

17. (#79-5932); Linda Greenhouse, "Parents Fight State Power to Deprive Them of Child," *New York Times*, 25 March 1980.

18. Ibid.

19. Doug Struck, "Which Mother Will Keep David? State Court of Appeals Must Decide," *Baltimore Sun*, 9 March 1980.

20. Ibid.

21. Ibid.

22. This paragraph, together with section 203 of Title II of the Child Abuse Prevention and Treatment and Adoption Reform Act of 1978, is identical in concept to the services provided by Arena (see chapter 2), which for over 12 years has been instrumental in hundreds of transracial adoptions and which participated in the effort to pass this act.

23. The range in 1980 for a family of four was $16,830 in Mississippi to $36,937 in Alaska. U.S. Senate, Committee on Finance, *Staff Data and Materials Relating to Social and Child Welfare Services*, table 4, "Federal Income Limits on Eligibility for Social Services," September 1979, pp. 40-41.

24. Ibid., table 5, "Estimated Distribution of Federal Funds among Selected Services," p. 42.

25. Ibid.

26. "Senate Votes Bill to Aid Placement of 'Hard-to-Place' Foster Children," *New York Times*, 30 October 1979.

27. *Staff Data and Materials Relating to Social and Child Welfare Services*, CP 96-29, p. 9.

28. Ibid., table II, "Child Welfare Services: State Estimates of Total Expenditures Reported under the Title IV-B, 'Programs from All Sources, Fiscal Year 1979' " pp. 50-51.

6 Intercountry Adoptions

Intercountry adoption is closely related to transracial adoption and has important implications for adoption in general. Because of social, religious, and political factors surrounding adoption, more and more prospective adoptive families (and individuals) are looking for healthy infants outside the United States. They find them in those countries whose policies permit foreign adoption agencies to take children out of orphanages and out of the country. In most cases, the decision to look outside the United States is not the couples' first course of action. Adoption from abroad becomes viable when adopters realize that "blue-ribbon" infants of any race are not available in the United States and that there is a three- to five-year wait for the *possibility* of adopting a healthy infant. Practically all intercountry adoptees to the United States are from nonwhite countries (primarily Asia and Latin America). Since the majority of adopters are white, these families will become the largest segment of the next generation of transracially adoptive families. This chapter reviews the current data on intercountry adoption and examines how it may affect transracial adoption.

It is often held that intercountry adoptions are made at the expense of permanent domestic placements. In other words, an American child might have been adopted if non-American-born infants were not available. Such an assertion overlooks the primary reason for the practice of intercountry adoption: the lack of adoptable, healthy infants in the United States and their comparatively greater availability abroad.[1] Intercountry adoption would not cease, however, even if the supply of adoptable American infants could satisfy all eligible adopters.

Arguments against intercountry adoptions resemble those against transracial adoption, both in rhetoric and effect. They question the morality of a family of one nationality (race) taking as their own a child from a different nationality (race). Some arguments equate intercountry adoption with white colonial exploitation of nonwhite peoples. In many respects, intercountry adoption is perceived as transracial-transcultural adoption.

Intercountry adoption gained American attention in a rather dramatic fashion. During the closing phases of our involvement in Southeast Asia, thousands of supposedly orphaned Vietnamese and Cambodian children were airlifted to the United States. Theoretically, most of them were to be adopted by American families.[2] The publicity surrounding the evacuation of these children aroused public sympathy and interest, although intercountry adoptions to the United States had been occuring since the end of World War II.[3] It was not until 1962 that the federal government began to collect figures on intercountry adoption. By 1978, the last year for which data are available, 47,007 foreign-born children were adopted by U.S. citizens.

A total of 29,003 non-American-born children were placed in the United States from 1962 through 1974. The airlift of Vietnamese children does not seem to have caused any extraordinary increase in the general trend. The number of children adopted into the United States from other countries had been increasing steadily by approximately 600 per year. Between 1974 and 1977, only about 400 more children per year were adopted into the United States, representing a modest and gradual increase. Although federal figures do not name the children's countries of origin, it is likely that between 1974 and 1977, intercountry adoptions were redistributed so that most children coming to the United States during this period were from Southeast Asia.

While intercountry adoption accounts for only a small percentage among all adoptions, table 6-2 shows intercountry adoption to be the only form of adoption on the increase. From 1968 to 1977, intercountry adoptions quadrupled from 1,612 to 6,493 per year. During almost the same period, 1968-1975, transracial adoptions increased only slightly from 733 to 831 per year.[4]

Intercountry adoption dropped somewhat from a near record of 6,493 in 1977 to 5,315 in 1978. This reduction was probably caused by several major "exporting" countries restricting international adoption. In 1978, Korea, Colombia, Ecuador, Costa Rica, Guatemala, El Salvador, Nicaragua, Liberia, and Sri Lanka all revised their adoption codes.[5]

There is little empirical data that examines the motivations of intercountry adopters. To assume that intercountry adoptions are made in lieu of domestic adoptions (particularly between 1974 and 1975 when intercountry adoptions increased from 4,770 to 5,663 and transracial adoption rose merely from 747 to 831), is to impugn the motives of those individuals who choose to adopt abroad.

The greatest number of children adopted into the United States come from Southeast Asia and the Republic of Korea (Korea). Large numbers are fathered by Americans. They are one of the most unfortunate legacies of our military involvements. These "Amerasian" children usually meet grim fates after their putative fathers return to the United States. Shunned by the extremely racially conscious societies of their mothers, they may be abandoned, placed in primitive orphanages, or, for the more fortunate ones, allowed to stay with their mothers in squalid conditions.[6]

In an article in the *New York Times Magazine*, Bill Kurtis described the desperate situation of these Amerasian children and the actions of 56 members of the U.S. Congress to raise their immigration status from

Table 6-1
Intercountry Adoptions, by Year

Year	1962[a]	1963	1964	1965	1966	1967	1968	1969	1970
Number of Adopters	385	1,312	1,651	1,448	1,679	1,905	1,602	2,080	2,409

Source: United States Department of Immigration and Naturalization, *Annual Reports* (Government Printing Office, Washington, D.C., 1962-1970).

[a] "Orphans Adopted Abroad or to be Adopted," Class established by Act, 26 September 1961.

Table 6-2
Intercountry Adoptions, Transracial Adoptions, Total Number of White Adoptions, Total Number of Adoptions, by Year, 1971-1978

	1971	1972	1973	1974	1975[e]	1976[f]	1977	1978
Total number of white adoptions[a]	147,000	59,158	71,940	54,095	56,977	(No data)		
Transracial adoptions[b]	2,574	1,569	1,091	747	831	1,070		(No data)
Intercountry adoptions[c]	2,724	3,023	4,015	4,770	5,633	6,552	6,493	5,315
Total number of adoptions (excluding TRA, ICA)[d]	169,000	99,552	113,042	107,874	104,188	(No data)		

[a]U.S. Department of Health, Education, and Welfare, publication (SRS) 76-03259, NCSS Report E-10 (1971-1975).
[b]*Opportunity*, The Boys and Girls Society of Oregon (30 December 1976).
[c]U.S. Department of Immigration and Naturalization, *Annual Reports* (Government Printing Office, Washington, D.C., 1962-1970).
[d]U.S. Department of Health, Education, and Welfare, publication (SRS) 76-03259.
[e]Last year for which national figures are available.
[f]Last year for which transracial adoption figures are available.

"nonpreference category," the lowest class of visa, to fourth preference (married sons and daughters of United States citizens) to first preference (unmarried sons and daughters of United States citizens).[7]

These children are estimated to number approximately 108,000. They are scattered throughout Korea and Southeast Asia: Japan, Okinawa, Taiwan, Thailand, Laos, Cambodia, the Philippines, and Vietnam.[8] However, they are not the only population from which prospective American adopters seek children. Many times children of two racially similar Oriental parents are available for adoption. We shall return to this topic later in our discussion.

Korean Adoptees

Korea was once considered a prime "exporter" of adoptable children. But in 1981 it had become quite difficult to adopt a Korean child.

Intercountry adoptions from Korea began on a modest scale in 1953, when the Seventh Day Adventists placed a few Korean children with American adopters. Religious organizations such as the Seventh Day Adventists, Catholic Relief Service, and Holt International Children's Services have dominated intercountry adoption since then.[9] These groups, as well as the International Social Service-Child Placement Service and the Korean Social Service, have found permanent foreign placements for approximately 12,384 Korean children.[10] The number of Korean children adopted abroad increased by 60 percent between 1968 and 1970 alone. This dramatic expansion was caused primarily by Western Europe, particularly Sweden, entering the market for Korea's children. In 1974 Holt International Children's Services placed 3,159 Korean children. By 1976 Holt had placed another 5,000 children as intercountry adoptees.[11] By 1976 approximately 16,000 Korean children had been adopted by Westerners, many of whom were Americans. That figure is about equal to the total number of transracial adoptions in the United States.

The number of incountry Korean adoptions is much smaller. Although Korea has a centuries-old adoption practice, it was conducted essentially for reasons of inheritance and ceremony (ancestral veneration) and restricted to males. Between 1962 and 1970, the first years in which Korean adoption figures were kept, about 9,971 incountry adoptions were made.[12] This is approximately 62 percent of the number of Korean children adopted internationally during those years.

In 1976 under pressure from other Asian countries, Korea reduced the number of overseas adoptions by 20 percent and announced its ultimate goal to curtail such placements entirely. The announced reduction, however, pertained only to full-blooded Korean children. Not included in the ban were children of mixed race, private intercountry adoptions, and handicapped children.[13]

The issue of racial purity in the Korean policy has had curious impact on intercountry adoption policies. Korea places much emphasis on racial purity, and the government has been known to commit overt acts of prejudice and discrimination against individuals of mixed blood.[14] It would appear that Korea would be more willing to export these children than those of full Korean parentage. But this is not the case. Although no accurate data are available, experts suggest that many more full-blooded Korean children have been adopted outside their country than have mixed-race children.[15] For example, 66 percent of the children that Holt placed internationally in 1968 were full-blooded Korean children. In 1970 the figure rose to 87 percent.[16] The Child Placement Service estimated that more than 75 percent of the females they placed for intercountry adoption had two Korean parents.[17] In 1970 these two organizations were responsible for placing some 80 percent of Korea's exported children. The Seventh Day Adventists and Korean Social Services accounted for the remaining 20 percent.[18]

The Immigration and Naturalization Service's most recent figures on intercountry adoption (1978) reflect the restriction of adoption policies in countries that traditionally supplied children to the United States. The trends suggest that intercountry adoption will not be as viable an alternative as it once was. Korea's statutes are not entirely consistent with these new policies since their export ban does not cover categories of children that are apparently still attractive to American adopters. In 1979 approximately 490 children were adopted in the state of Maryland. Seventy of these were intercountry adoptions: 37 were Korean, 25 Latin American, 7 Indian, and 1 from Bangladesh.[19]

It is unlikely that all 70 of these intercountry adoptees were healthy infants, born of two racially similar parents. The lack of data notwithstanding, a percentage of these children were probably either physically and/or emotionally handicapped, of mixed parentage, or beyond infancy. These characteristics did not stand in the way of their adoption by American families.

If Maryland is representative, we may deduce that those countries traditionally supplying children to the United States will resume such action after an initial drop in the number of intercountry adoptions. Restrictive policies may initially reduce the number of available children and switch the focus to a different type such as handicapped. After a short interval, however, the number of international adoptees, both hard to place and not hard to place, may return to the 1977 level.

Response of the Child Welfare League to Intercountry Adoption

The CWLA sets the most influential standards in the field of child welfare. Its pronouncements on such matters as foster care, group homes, child protection, institutional care, daycare, and homemaker service, are not binding on agencies and institutions, but CWLA statements on child-welfare-related issues carry considerable weight.

With regard to intercountry adoption, CWLA follows its own some-what cautious and conservative philosophy.[20] CWLA has stated that inter-country adoption should not be considered until all other possible child-placement alternatives have been exhausted within the child's country of origin. Without mentioning any one geographical area of the world, CWLA recognizes that social integration within the birth culture is the most impor-tant issue for mixed-race children. CWLA cautions that intercountry adop-tion should be considered a placement of "last resort."

> Intercountry adoptive placements should be considered for the child whose development, *family or social background* (authors' emphasis) present in-surmountable handicaps to his acceptance, care, and optimum adjustment in his own country.
>
> . . . If emigration and adoption are likely to bring economic and social ad-vantages to the child, these advantages should be weighed against the psychological and legal consequences of an inter-country adoption.[21]

The CWLA is concerned with two main issues: legal safeguards both for the internationally adopted child and for his/her American adoptive parents;[22] and establishment of the social-work procedures to ensure an appropriate placement for each child:

> Once adoption in the United States is considered to be in a child's best in-terests, the same safeguards should apply for such a child as for native born children adopted in this country. These safeguards include protection and social services for the natural parents, the child, and the adoptive parents. . . .[23]

CWLA is not in total sympathy with the prospect of largescale intercoun-try placement,[24] but it has nevertheless issued a set of guidelines designed to protect all participants in this type of adoption.

Intercountry Adoption and the Model State Adoption Act

In the section on intercountry adoption, the Model State Adoption Act reads,

> There appears to be no equivocation that inter-country adoption is anything but a practical and legitimate method of family planning.[25]

The act suggests that all children adopted in foreign lands by American citizens be "readopted in the United States for reasons of comity."[26] Follow-ing are some aspects of intercountry adoption covered in the act:

1. Individual states "must provide postadoption services (by public agencies) for applicants or arrange for services by voluntary agencies."[27]

2. The Immigration and Naturalization Service must be satisfied that the state's preadoption requirements have been met for each intercountry adoption.

    The INS requires family assessments for inter-country placements, and the Act requires that an agency provide postplacement services.[28]

3. The adoptive family assessment for inter-country adoptions (is the responsibility of the adoption agency). . . . There should be greater emphasis on the educative function, so that families are aware of what information they should obtain about the child, his background, culture, and country of origin.[29]

The commentaries appended to the act explain and illustrate many sections and subsections of the act. Like the act, they do not question the validity of intercountry adoption. The commentaries note that individual states must verify that the biological parent(s) ceded parental rights in accordance with the laws of the child's country of origin:

> State officials must ascertain that the evidence of termination of parental rights according to the laws of the child's country of origin is sufficient for the adoption to be complete once the child arrives. . . .
>
> Evidence of termination of parental rights must . . . be filed along with the petition for adoption, and the court must find that termination has occurred prior to issuing a decree of adoption.[30]

Recommendations of the Children's Bureau

In conjunction with the American Public Welfare Association (APWA) and assisted by a 22-member advisory committee, the Children's Bureau launched a project in 1977 to develop a set of recommendations

> which specifically relate to the provision of services by public authorities and the private sector, and to the administrative mechanisms that facilitate the process of intercountry adoption.[31]
>
> [The Children's Bureau] has a long-standing commitment to ensuring that children and families in the United States receive needed protections and safeguards during the adoption process (and) recognized a compelling need to afford the same protections to foreign born children adopted by Americans. This need for guidance was brought to the Bureau's attention by many states that were seeking to provide services to an ever-expanding number of parents and children involved in intercountry adoption. The Bureau was aware of the unique characteristics and complexities of the international adoption process and believed there was a need to encourage more consistent service and administrative practices nationwide.[32]

Their work culminated in 1979 with the publication of *Intercountry Adoption Guidelines* (the Guidelines), a 101-page document dealing with most issues relevant to intercountry adoptions.[33] Following the Model State Adoption Act and the Standards for Adoption Service of CWLA, the Guidelines emphasize the legal aspects of intercountry adoption as defined by the Immigration and Naturalization Service.[34] All concerned agencies want to avoid repeating the large-scale adoption of Southeast Asian children that occurred after the fall of Vietnam and Cambodia. Because of the confusion surrounding the event, parents and close relatives later appeared in the United States to reclaim their children from their new adoptive families.[35]

The Guidelines also treat the functions and responsibilities of various federal and state child-welfare agencies as they relate to intercountry adoption.

The Guidelines do not attempt to link intercountry adoption with domestic adoption, nor do they suggest that an American-born child's chances of adoption are jeopardized by intercountry adoption.

One of the most pressing issues confronting both private and governmental child-welfare agencies is the large number of children in foster care who have little hope of being reunited with their biological families. Contrary to its intent, foster care has become a permanent situation for many children. Several measures have been taken to disentangle these children from a system incapable of providing stability.

1. Subsidized adoption is now available so that adoptive individuals receive financial assistance when they adopt certain categories of children.
2. Mandated foster-care reviews occur after a given period of time (usually two years) if children are not reunited with their parents or if other permanent plans have not been made. Parental rights are abrogated by the court, and the child is placed in the "adoptable" category.
3. Special units of some agencies or individual agencies have been organized to deal specifically with the adoption of hard-to-place children.

These policies and programs have been developed only recently. They are intended to settle the problems of parentless children adrift in various child-care systems. But these problems are so enormous and of such long standing that few results are yet apparent.

A 1978 report, *National Study of Social Services to Children and Their Families*,[36] prepared for the Children's Bureau, noted that "of the approximately one half million children known to be in foster care, 100,000 were free for adoption, of whom 40 percent were non-white and another 40 percent were 11 years old or above." Twenty-two percent of those children

(110,000) had had foster care recommended as their *permanent placement*. An equal percentage had been in foster care for six or more years. This is evidence that foster care has burgeoned into an unintended service-delivery system.

The financial cost of foster care is staggering. Of the $2.3 billion spent annually by state and federal agencies on all child-welfare services, more than one half ($1.117 billion) is allocated for foster care.[37] Between 1974 and 1977, the per-child cost to the federal government rose from $1,000 to $1,800.[38]

Once again it would appear that if intercountry adoption were not possible, the great majority of prospective adopters still would not view domestic adoption as a viable alternative.

A 1978 CWLA survey provided some interesting and challenging responses.[39] Ninety percent of the prospective adoptive parents indicated that they would have "major reservations" about adopting white children with noncorrectable handicaps; for older black children, the figure was 97 percent; and with older children of other ethnic groups, it was 80 percent. Sixty-one percent of the prospective parents said they could *not* adopt a white child with a noncorrectable handicap, 85 percent could not adopt an older black child, and 66 percent could not adopt an older child of another ethnic group. Seventy-six percent of the adopters indicated that if given an opportunity to adopt a healthy white child older than six years, they would have major reservations or could not adopt (28 percent and 48 percent, respectively). Perhaps even more startling was the fact that 36 percent of the respondents revealed similar views about healthy white children above the age of two. Based on this study, it would appear that most of the 100,000 children currently available for adoption will not find permanent settings.

We do not believe that intercountry adoption poses any threat to domestic adoption at this time. Placement opportunities for native-born adoptable children are not jeopardized by the current rate of intercountry adoption. The parents for whom intercountry adoption is a serious if not sole option probably would not be attracted to the American children presently available for adoption. These individuals desire healthy infants, and they will not be available for adoption in any numbers in the foreseeable future.

Fifty-six percent of the respondents to the CWLA survey indicated that they could adopt an Oriental, Native-American, or Chicano infant with only minor reservations. Only 13 percent expressed the same willingness toward normal black infants.[40] These responses support our contention that domestic adoptees are not jeopardized by intercountry adoption. When given a choice between adopting native-born black or ethnic infants, most adoptive couples choose the latter. The data indicates that if more native-born ethnic children were available for adoption, international adoption would probably diminish greatly. The choice is not available today, however, because most adoption agencies do not recommend transracial adoptions.

With the cooperation of FACE (Families Adopting Children Everywhere), we surveyed their member families who have adopted children from other countries. FACE is an adoptive parents' organization, not an adoption agency. It disseminates "support, encouragement, and information" to prospective adopters and to adoptive parents via a monthly newsletter and local meetings. The questionnaires contained the same items that we used in the second phase of our study on transracial adoption, supplemented by questions seeking background information such as we had collected from our families in 1972. The Open Door Society and the Council on Adoptable Children supplied us with our original group of names.

FACE agreed to attach our questionnaire to their newsletter. Eighty of the 159 names on the mailing list were active members, that is, families who had adopted transracially. Of those 80 families, about 40 percent had children within the age categories that we were studying: between ten and sixteen years. We received 22 responses, representing about 69 percent of those eligible. Thirteen of these 22 families had completed intercountry adoptions.

The social characteristics of FACE members differ significantly from the families in our original sample in at least one way. Religion seems to play a more important role in the lives of the FACE families. They are more active churchgoers, and they use religious symbols in describing their emotions and motivations. Of the 22 families who responded, 18 attend Protestant or Catholic churches at least once a week. The churches to which they belong include Morman, Baptist, Jehovah's Witness, Catholic, Unitarian, and Lutheran. Like the families in our major survey, these fathers hold professional positions or are in business for themselves. Fifteen of the 22 families had children born to them before they adopted. With one or two exceptions, the families live in all-white neighborhoods.

The FACE respondents also are different in that the majority (13 out of the 22) had adopted transnationally as well as transracially, most of the children were more than five years old at the time they were adopted, and most adopted Korean children; some adopted Vietnamese and others East Indian children.

When asked why they adopted the types of children they did, most parents answered that they were interested in providing homes for hard-to-place children, and these were the children available. Others thought they would be more comfortable with a Korean child than an American black and suggested they would have an easier time raising the foreign-born child, "Adopting a foreign child is different from adopting a black child. A black child is from American society. Interestingly, they suffer from prejudice, which is not usually the case with a foreign child.'' For those families who adopted older children, Korean and Vietnamese children were probably more accessible than American black or American Indian children. This is due to the fact that most states did not permit the adoption of black or Indian children by white parents by the mid-1970s.

The families share a sense of well-being. Many of them use the term ''blessed'' in describing themselves. It seems appropriate. They view their adopted children as ''gifts from God.'' In describing their third daughter (their first adopted child), one mother wrote, ''A is our third precious gift from our Heavenly Father.'' Another parent wrote, ''We want a large family, and we feel this is how God wants us to become one.'' Another parent wrote, ''Our home is blessed because our girls are here with us. I feel God has given them to us as surely as if they were born to us.''

Sixteen of the 22 families checked our item, ''basically positive and good,'' to describe their relationships with their adopted children. The other six families checked, ''There are problems but the positive elements outweigh the negative ones.'' Within this category, one family reported that their adopted black daughter ''had been stealing money from other family members and lying to cover it up.'' The other four sisters, all of whom were born to the parents, responded with anger and annoyance and told their parents they wished they had not adopted her.

Other families felt the adopted child was having difficulty fitting into the family because he or she had been adopted recently or after he or she was seven years old. One family adopted twelve children, in addition to three that were born to them. They described problems with one of their black adopted sons: ''He had been shoved out of an adopted home after nine years and finalization. He has many insecurities and behavior problems.'' Another family that adopted four children and had three born to them described problems with the black daughter they had adopted at an older age. She is now ten, but she had not had a permanent home until she was adopted at the age of seven. ''Her insecurities and her need for attention and affection are greater than the other children's.'' Similar comments were made by a family who adopted a Korean boy when he was seven years old. They had adopted two other children when they were six and seven weeks old, with whom they were having no problems.

Grow and Shapiro found that ''about one fourth of the parents reported problems stemming from the fact that the child was older when entering their home and presented difficulties because of her or his earlier life experiences.''[41] The pattern of difficulties with older children did not surface in our major survey because over 80 percent of our families had adopted infants or children under three years of age.

The families who had adopted children from more ''exotic'' cultures (in the sense that there were great differences between the parents' world and that of the children) were more likely to rear them as Americans. They were less likely to help the children retain memories, feelings, or knowledge about Korean or Vietnamese language, customs, history, food, or holiday observances. Some of the parents wrote that their adopted children were not interested in their Korean or Vietnamese heritage, were not familiar with Korean or Vietnamese customs, identified as Americans, and felt part of their new communities. When the families served Vietnamese or Korean food, the children were apt to resent it. A few of the parents who had adopted older children wrote that their children's only memory of Korea or Vietnam was the orphanages in which they had stayed until adopted. An orphanage is not part of the mainstream of any society. Their children, they said, felt stigmatized and inferior. Their children's memories were not happy ones. The children wanted to leave behind that part of life and become fully integrated into American society. In that spirit, one parent wrote, "I expect my children to live in a community similar to ours—middle class, largely white—they've had enough changes." To such children, adoption represents not only emotional security and physical well-being but also stability. The wandering and homelessness is over.

In adopting foreign children, the parents feel that they are cooperating in their children's efforts to burn their bridges. The children have no option but to adapt to their new world. There is no going back.

This situation is in sharp contrast to the family that adopts a black child. The American black child has the option of returning. Indeed, that option may be the more realistic one, according to many social workers and adoption-agency personnel. Difficult as it may be for a black child reared in a transracial family to share the mainstream black experience, society perceives him as belonging to that black experience and expects him to share it.

According to their parents, almost all the Korean, East Indian, and Vietnamese children identify themselves as Americans, or white, or as "hyphenated Americans." Most have white friends and are expected to live in communities much like the ones in which they are being raised. The parents expect them to be accepted by white society—especially by middle or upper-middle-class whites. One parent said of her East Indian son, "I believe that he will probably integrate beautifully into American society." Another mother wrote about her children's Vietnamese, Indian, and Korean identities, "It's hard to say yet—they each know their country and their race, but they are being raised as white, because that's what our community is. If we ask them where they are from, they say Saigon, etc., but 'What are you?' is answered 'American' or 'Vietnamese American.'"

The parents of adopted American black children report that their children identify themselves as black. The parents anticipate that when they grow up, they are not likely to live in the same social world as their parents or white siblings. They anticipate their children's need to live in an integrated community or perhaps in a black community. This supports earlier observations that adopting a child of another culture (especially if that culture is far away) may be less problematic and complicated and involve less adjustment than adopting an American black child, especially if the adoptee is an infant.

Among these families, adoption of a nonwhite child aroused almost no hostility or rejection by grandparents and other relatives. The relatives of the FACE families were more approving and supportive of the adoption than those of our major survey. One family wrote that they "achieved instant sainthood" in the eyes of their relatives and neighbors because they took a child out of an orphanage. Another wrote, "Friends and relatives are intrigued—I enjoy a rather unique status." Several respondents reported that they were not the first in their families to adopt transracially but that siblings or other relatives had led the way. While none of the families suffered permanent estrangement, some talked of mothers or fathers who were uncomfortable and ill at ease with their new grandchildren "especially when they come in two's or three's and were not babies." Some respondents said their parents hoped that adoption would not keep them from having more children. Such families were concerned because their married children practiced birth control, contrary to their religious beliefs, and felt that they adopted only to justify that transgression.

None of the respondents felt that the transracial adoption had placed a strain on their marriages. Those parents with large families (six or more children) described problems of finding time to relate to each other. They were characterized as "strategic" rather than as emotionally difficult matters. The father of five adopted children (and one biological child) wrote,

> The problems each new child brought made us redefine our sense of values sometimes with surprising results. Now the sheer volume of people we deal with makes it difficult to keep our one-to-one relationship in focus. We have learned to make time for each other and not apologize for it. We have also learned to allow for more individual pursuits rather than joint or group efforts.

Another parent wrote,

> Well you could hardly become the parent of seven children (four of whom were adopted) and not have it affect your relationship with your spouse—after all, there are only so many hours in a day. We don't get out by ourselves very often and a lot of energy is spent on children—maybe it makes the time we have together by ourselves just that more special.

About their own personalities or self-definition several respondents wrote,

Becoming the parent of all these children has helped me become (I hope) a more mature well-rounded person. It's like finally realizing exactly what I wanted to do with my life.

I'm terrific. That hasn't changed.

I feel I am stronger. I define myself as a white woman with black children.

I am happier, more fulfilled, proud of being his mother—completed.

One of the last items on our questionnaire asked:

If a family in this community, like your own in terms of religious background, income, and education, asked you to advise them about whether they ought to adopt a nonwhite child, what specifically would you advise them to do?

We asked the question in our first survey, and 90 percent responded that they would urge the family to go ahead and adopt. Grow and Shapiro reported that 91 percent of their respondents answered in the same way.[42] The parents wanted to communicate the importance of love and the selfish desire to have a child. High-sounding, unselfish, generous motives, a desire to change the world, the public expression of liberalism, and lack of prejudice all were the wrong reasons for adoption.

The FACE respondents all urged transracial adoption for pretty much the same reasons. Those who had adopted older children expressed greater caution. One family warned about health problems and the burden of paperwork. Another set of parents who had adopted their children when they were four, five, and ten years old, after having six children born to them, advised, "I'd ask them to explore their feelings about the race of people in general. To ask themselves if they feel that all Orientals are gooks, except the children they want to adopt; are all blacks lazy?"

Some emphasized the immensity of the commitment. One parent wrote,

I would recommend it—but they should be very sure in their own minds that this is what they want and can cope with every aspect of it, since this is a lifelong commitment on everyone's part and not something you try and see if it works out.

Another parent wrote,

Explore your very inner feelings of love. It takes strength and you have to be strong enough to handle stress in all areas of life—marriage, other children, religion, family, friends, business. It requires more than talk and a lot of doing.

The strongest statement contained this advice:

> Be motivated—be willing if necessary to terminate all existing relationships: e.g. parents, friends. Commit themselves to continuous residence in a multiracial community.

Two of the families mentioned the positive effect that the transracial adoption had on their biological children. Their children became indifferent to race as a basis of evaluation. One mother wrote of her eleven- and twelve-year-old biological children and their choice of friends, "Only when the 'new kid' is brought home do I find out that he/she is Korean, Black, Mexican, etc."

Another commented, "We have found that since we have experienced interracial and handicapped adoption, not only are our children more tolerant of other people's differences, but also so are those who come in contact with our family."

A theme heard frequently from our larger set of families and one that was repeated among the FACE families concerned the importance of involving the siblings in the decision to adopt. To be successful, adoption must be a family decision. Emphasizing this point, a father discussed the benefits of adoption with their biological children. He wrote, "Our older (biological) children have given up something—time, energy, money, to have a large family. Our younger children (including the adopted ones) have given up their culture to become part of ours. But in every way, there is only addition to each life." From the family that adopted twelve children, "I would not live any other way."

Notes

1. Prospective adoptive parents in the United States are in competition with adoptive parents from Western Europe, where there is also a dearth of adoptable infants. A 1977 report indicated that children from Thailand, bought by baby brokers in Thailand for $50 each, were resold for $2,500 to adoptive parents in Sweden, Britain, and West Germany (*Baltimore Sun*, 15 April 1977, p. 3). The current price for an available infant of two white parents in the United States is $25,000. (*New York Times*, 28, June 1977, p. 1.)

2. For a fuller discussion, see Rita Simon and Howard Altstein, *Transracial Adoption* (Wiley Interscience, New York, 1977), chapter 3.

3. Helen Miller, "Korean International Children," *Lutheran Social Welfare* (Summer 1971):12-23.

4. For an excellent discussion of intercountry adoption, see Barbara Joe, "In Defense of Inter-country Adoption," *Social Service Review* 52 (No. 1) (March 1978):20.

5. Ibid.

6. A tragic example of the plight of these children is illustrated in Thailand. In 1972 Thailand enacted the following statute: "Thai nationality shall be withdrawn from any person born of a foreign father or mother, or of a father residing in the country temporarily." In 1978 it was estimated that approximately 4,000 Thai-born children had American fathers. In effect, these are stateless children. Deprived of identity cards or passports, they are forbidden to enroll in a university, own property, leave the country, or engage in civilian or military service. Even refugee status is denied them [*International Child Welfare Review* 38-39 (September-December 1978):6].

7. P.O. Box 102, Bel Air, MO 21014, September 1979; Bill Kurtis, "The Plight of Children Abandoned in Vietnam," *New York Times Magazine*, 2 March 1980, p. 18.

8. Kurtis, "The Plight of Children Abandoned in Vietnam."

9. Since the end of U.S. involvement in Vietnam, other groups, mostly religious, have been active in caring for parentless Asian children and participating in intercountry adoptions. They include the American Red Cross, Catholic Relief Services, U.S. Catholic Conference, International Rescue Committee, Church World Service, the American Council for Nationalities, Lutheran Immigration and Refugee Service, World Relief Refugee Services, and the Pearl S. Buck Foundation (Kurtis, "The Plight of Children Abandoned in Vietnam").

10. For an excellent examination of this topic, see Miller, "Korean International Children."

11. Joe, "In Defense of Intercountry Adoption," footnote 33.

12. Miller, "Korean International Children," footnote 7, p. 21.

13. Joe, "In Defense of Intercountry Adoption," footnotes 34 and 54, pp. 18-19.

14. In 1970, for example, a leading newspaper in Seoul stated that the government was about to exempt mixed-race males from the armed services on racial grounds. The government never recanted the story. (Miller, "Korean International Children," p. 13.)

15. Ibid., p. 14.

16. Ibid.

17. It is interesting to note that many more females than males have been adopted outside their shores. This is probably due to the fact that males are considered more desirable in Korean society and are much less frequently abandoned.

18. Miller, "Korean International Children," p. 15.

19. *FACE Facts* (Bel Air, Md.) July 1979.

20. Child Welfare League of America (CWLA), *Standards for Adoption Service*, Section 7.43-7.48, pp. 116-120. CWLA guidelines on intercountry adoption were developed in conjunction with the U.S. Department of Health, Education and Welfare Children's Bureau.

21. Ibid., pp. 116-117.

22. Ibid.; see, in particular, the sections, "Immigration Law and Procedures" and "Legal Aspects."

23. Ibid., pp. 116-117.

24. During the height of the Vietnam emergency evacuation, CWLA issued a statement calling upon all concerned to stop the "uprooting" of these children. Other child-welfare groups issued similar statements ("American Aid Needed to Keep Vietnamese Children in Vietnam," press release, Children's Welfare League of America, New York, 4 April 1975).

25. U.S. Department of Health, Education and Welfare, "Model State Adoption Act and Model State Adoption Procedures," *Federal Register* 45 (No. 33) (15 February 1980).

26. "Model State Adoption Act," p. 10025.

27. Ibid., p. 10727.

28. Ibid., p. 10628.

29. Ibid.

30. Ibid., p. 10660.

31. "Inter-country Adoption Guidelines," U.S. Department of Health, Education and Welfare, Office of Human Development Services, Administration for Children, Youth, and Families, Children's Bureau, DHEW Publications (OHDS) 80-30251 (Government Printing Office, Washington, D.C., March 1980), p. vii.

32. Ibid.

33. Ibid.

34. The names and addresses of state and local agencies, along with local parent groups specializing in intercountry adoptions, appear in a separate document compiled by the Children's Bureau and APWA in conjunction with the guidelines [U.S. Department of Health, Education and Welfare, Office of Human Development, Administration for Children, Youth, and Families, Children's Bureau, *National Directory of Intercountry Adoption Service Resources*, DHEW Publications (OHDS) 80-30252 (Government Printing Office, Washington, D.C., March 1980)].

35. See Simon and Altstein, *Transracial Adoption*, chapter 3, p. 64.

36. Shyne and Schroeder, *National Study of Social Services To Children and Their Families*, Children's Bureau, DHEW Publications (Washington, D.C.: Government Printing Office, August 1980).

37. U.S. Government Accounting Office, *Facts Regarding Subsidized Adoptions*, Washington, D.C., 1978, pp. 3-4.

38. Ibid., p. 5.

39. William Meezan, Sanford Katz, and Eva Manoff Russo, *Adoptions Without Agencies: A Study of Independent Adoptions* (Child Welfare League of America, New York, 1978).

40. Ibid., table 5-1, p. 85.

41. Lucille J. Grow and Deborah Shapiro, *Black Children—White Parents: A Study of Transracial Adoption* (Child Welfare League of America, New York, 1974), p. 88.

42. Ibid., p. 86.

7 Concluding Remarks

We conclude by returning to the themes with which we introduced this volume. We emphasize again that our account of the parents' sense of the family's togetherness and well-being, of their perceptions about how well the transracial adoption has succeeded, and their views about their children's racial identities are tentative and limited to a particular period in the family's life. We selected this period because the transracially adopted children were about to enter adolescence or were already young teenagers. We felt this was a propitious time to take a second reading. When we first encountered these families in 1972, the children's ages ranged from three to eight, and most of the transracially adopted members of the family were less than six years old. Rather than launch a full-scale survey of the children and the parents, we contacted only the parents and asked them to serve as respondents. We hope to interview the children and their parents three or four years from now when most of the children will be finishing high school.

As we review what we have learned from this survey, it is clear that the extraordinarily glowing, happy portrait that we painted seven years ago now has some blemishes on it. It shows some signs of stress and tension. For every five families in which there are the usual pleasures and joys along with sibling rivalries, school-related problems, and difficulties in communication between parent and child, there is one family whose difficulties are more profound and are believed by the parents to be directly related to the transracial adoption.

The serious problem that the parents cite most frequently is the adopted children's (usually it is a boy) tendencies to steal from other members of their families. We have described parents' accounts of how bicycles, clothing, and money had been stolen from siblings rooms and that brothers and sisters had resorted to putting locks on their bedroom doors. Another serious problem is the parents' rather painful discoveries that the adopted children had physical, mental, or emotional disabilities that are either genetic or were the result of indifferent or abusive treatment the children received in foster homes. The one real tragedy among our families is the child suffering from phenylketonuria (PKU). When we contacted her parents this time, we learned that C had been placed in a state institution. But like the first encounter, the father is still more positive and optimistic than the mother. In this last interview, the father said that he thought C was improving and might one day be able to relate to her family in a warm and loving manner. In addition to this extreme situation, there are also a handful of parents who are bitter toward and resentful of their social workers or adoption agencies, or simply at the way things have worked out. They had asked for and thought they had received healthy babies, and they learned within a few years that the children had learning disabilities, were diabetic, or had serious emotional problems. The parents believe that the agencies took advantage of them by purposely withholding important information or by providing false information about the children. It is important to emphasize, however, as we did earlier in the text, that not all the parents who discovered that their adopted children had genetic physical or mental problems were bitter and resentful. Those who are not bitter view the problem as still another challenge to be dealt with constructively and optimistically.

Still a third theme of discontent focused on parental guilt. A few parents felt that by adopting a child of another race they had caused pain or inflicted harm on the child or children who had been born to them. The pain was the result either of neglect because integrating a child of a different race into the family had absorbed so much of their time and energy as not to leave enough for the other children, or because the family had so rearranged its life style that the child born into the family felt estranged and left out.

Although we have pointed out the warts and the blemishes in transracial adoptions, we have not found that negative feelings and disappointments outweigh or even come close to characterizing the large majority of the families' experiences. Indeed, most of the parents reported that their adoption experiences had brought happiness, commitment, and fulfillment to their lives. Among the twenty-three single-parent families, almost all the mothers and fathers emphasized that the transracial adoptions had enriched their lives and that the tensions and pain leading to the separations or divorces were not related to the adoptions. The majority of the parents still feel, as they did seven years ago, that their decisions to adopt transracially were among the wisest and most satisfying they had ever made. The children not only provide enormous intrinsic value but they also provide the parents with another window through which to view the world. Simply put, they help make the parents' lives more varied, more interesting, and more challenging. Having a black son or an Indian daughter sets them apart; and most of the parents enjoy their special status. Most of them also believe that it is healthy for the other children in their families. It gives them a broader base from which to view and participate in the human experience.

Some of these themes came through with great clarity among the FACE families, many of whom have adopted children from Vietnam, India, Latin America, and other parts of the world.

Completing this book at the beginning of 1981, we note that transracial adoption has not been completely stymied as we feared it would be in 1975.

But the number of such adoptions continues to be small, and the trend shows no sign of turning upward. Even with the combined efforts of black social workers and child-care agencies, thousands of children remain in institutions awaiting adoption, the majority of whom are black. In recent years the state courts have not acted consistenty in supporting or opposing transracial adoptions, and the state legislatures and executive departments have by and large ignored the problem.

We end this volume as we did the earlier one by emphasizing that the story about the families in our survey is not finished and the problem of homeless children living out their childhoods in institutions has not been resolved. We hope that there is a relationship between how well the children in our families turn out; how adjusted, how happy, and how emotionally secure they are, and the policies that are adopted to reduce the number of homeless children.

Appendix A
Open Records: The
Right to Know

No discussion of adoption would be complete without considering one of the most sensitive issues being debated today: the extent to which adult adoptees should have access to their own background information. This includes the delicate matter of the unsealing of court records and other documents without jeopardizing the biological parents' right to privacy. In the parlance of social work, this is referred to as an adoptee's "right to know."

We do not intend to analyze the complex legalities surrounding the issue of an adoptee's right to know. These have been reviewed extensively already![1] Rather, this appendix summarizes the development of the right-to-know movement and examines what effect, if any, it has had on trans-racially adopted individuals.

In an era of increased sensitivity and awareness of one's ethnic and racial identity, it is not surprising that adoptees would also desire a fuller understanding of their identities. Adoptees, however, represent a distinct group. For the past half-century, they have been restricted from access to any information on their personal backgrounds prior to adoption, let alone any material regarding ethnic and racial heritage. It is as if they do not exist prior to their "rebirth" through adoption.

Only four states permit adult adoptees to examine their original birth certificates.[2] The other 46 states all have statutes that regulate, in varying degrees, an adult adoptee's access to his or her birth records. New York, California, Oklahoma, and Utah have legislation pending that would allow adoptees' access.[3]

Currently the only federal legislation addressing the issue of open records, even to a limited degree, is the Indian Child Welfare Act of 1978, which deals solely with matters involving Native Americans.[4] This legislation allows all Native American adoptees over the age of eighteen access to the tribal identification of their biological parent(s). This provision is included in the law in order to prevent the adoptees from being denied any tribal rights to which they may be entitled. The law, however, does not allow any personal information to be released pertaining to the identities, whereabouts, and so on of the biological parents.[5]

Other countries such as Israel, Finland, and Scotland have for some time allowed adult adoptees access to their birth records. In 1975 England passed the Children's Act, permitting an adult adoptee to review his or her birth records.[6]

Adoption has historically been synonymous with secrecy in the name of confidentiality, and there was a certain logic to this relationship. Throughout the history of adoption in the United States, agencies generally saw the adoptive parents as their primary clients. The agencies defined their goal as finding children for families rather than families for children. Once an adoption was finalized, the record of proceedings was sealed by statute. The statutes were designed to protect the rights and anonymity of each party in the adoption triangle: the adoptee, the adopter, and the biological parent(s). Again, a certain logic prevailed. If all records were inaccessible to all participants, everyone was assured that the past would not intrude on the present. The biological parent(s), having surrendered the child for whatever reason, would not have to fear being confronted one day by an individual demanding to know of events best forgotten. For adoptive parents and adoptees, sealed records were reasonable assurance that they too would not come face to face with an inquiring biological parent wanting to see his or her child and asking similarly uncomfortable questions. Sealed records also precluded one of the greatest anxieties of adoptive parents: that an adopted child would have to make a choice between adoptive and biological parents, should such an encounter occur.

The same mid-1970s era that saw an awakening of interest in "roots" also witnessed the development of several nationwide and state organizations working to repeal statutes sealing adoptees' birth records. These groups developed around two fundamental issues: personal identity and genealogy. Nationwide organizations such as Adoptees' Liberty Movement Association (ALMA) and Orphans Voyage and state associations such as Search for Tomorrow (Indiana), Adoptees' Identity Movement (Michigan), Adoptees as Adults (Oklahoma), and the Washington Adoptees' Rights Movement (Washington) are all devoted to unsealing adult adoptees' birth records.[7]

Legal Rationale

Since ancient times laws have recognized a strong link between adoption as a form of rebirth and the denial of events prior to adoption to all concerned (especially the adoptee). Babylonian law, through the Code of Hammurabi, required the removal of an adoptee's tongue and eyes, lest that individual publically disclose his or her adopted status or attempt to seek out his or her biological parents.[8]

Roman law favored adoptive parents and called for an involved religious ceremony symbolizing the end of one life (prior to adoption) and the beginning of another (rebirth).[9]

Although English Common Law is the basis for much of America's legal system, it did not deal with adoption until 1926. Massachusetts passed America's first adoption law in 1851. French adoption law (modeled on Roman law and the Justinian Code) strongly affected some of the earliest adoption legislation in the United States.[10]

It was not until the mid-1940s that adoption professionals redefined their functions and began to view the adoptee—and not the adoptive family—as the primary client. This change caused a greater emphasis on secrecy and confidentiality,[11] which in turn was reflected in adoption laws and practice. They were not too dissimilar from the findings of a British court in 1956:

> In general, it is the policy of the law to make the veil between the past and present lives of adopted persons as opaque and inpenetrable as possible, like the veil which God has placed between the living and the dead.[12]

Twenty-five years later, in a much different world, Carolyn Burke summarized majority legal opinion when she wrote,

> The adult adoptee has a right of access to his original birth certificate, because denial of this information by the state is a violation of his First Amendment right to receive information and his constitutional right to privacy. Although the state's interest in establishing and preserving the adoptive process justifies denial of access while the adoptee is a child, this interest cannot sustain the denial once the adoptee has become an adult. Moreover, the natural parents' privacy interests are not of constitutional proportions and can be sufficiently protected through existing tort law for invasions of privacy.

> Opening the birth records to the adoptee when he becomes of age should have salutary effects on the adoptive process. Official recognition of the adoptee's right to his birth certificate may alleviate the feelings of guilt and shame created by the secrecy now associated with the sealed records. Also, the knowledge that the original birth certificate will be available to the adopted child when he becomes an adult may encourage adoptive parents to provide him with more information about his natural parents during childhood. Most importantly, the recognition of the adoptee's right of access to the original birth certificate will relieve the many adults who feel the need or desire to search for their origins from the procedural burdens and obstructions they now have to face.[13]

Organizational/Institutional Response

Most social agencies and professional organizations involved in adoption either have issued public statements on the adoptee's right to know or have developed a policy toward it.

At its 1979 convention, the Delegate Assembly of the NASW issued the following statement regarding open records.

> The adoptee's right-to-know and the limits of confidentiality to which the parties to adoption now are subject must be addressed.
>
> The needs and right of adoptees to know their birth origins should be recognized. This right (includes) requests from adult adoptees for identifying information. . . . The social work profession, along with social agencies, has a responsibility to initiate and support appropriate changes in the law that would facilitate sharing on identifying information between adult adoptees and birth parents when both parties are in agreement.[14]

Clearly the NASW supports an adult adoptee's right to know, provided the birth parents' rights to anonymity are not jeopardized. This caveat is included in practically all statutes and public statements regarding open records.

The CWLA deals with this sensitive issue in one sentence. Under the title of "Social Work Services Following Adoptive Placement: Disclosure of Identifying Information about the Natural Parents to Adopted Adults," it states:

> Information that identifies the natural parents should be given to the adopted adult who requests it when ordered by the court, or if legislation permits disclosure, when authorized by the natural parents who relinquished the child.[15]

The preceding statement is considerably changed from the CWLA's 1973 position, which stressed the confidential nature of adoption, reaffirmed the traditional principle of anonymity among all concerned, and states that birth parents

> should not be involved after the relinquishment of the child; and that the child should be protected . . . from the intervention of the natural parents after his placement.[16]

The Model State Adoption Act and Commentaries also cover this issue. Although an adult adoptee's right to know is only mentioned in the act,

> The law requires that the records of the agency and the court compiled in any proceedings covered by the Act be retained for 99 years after the child reaches the age of majority. *Retention assures the material will be available in future years to adult adoptees, birth parents, and adoptive parents.* (emphasis added)

In a subsequent paragraph dealing with birth records, the act continues,

> The original certificate remains sealed to the adoptee until he attains majority, at which time he may inspect the original record, which contains the names of his birth parents.[17]

Taken together, these paragraphs indicate that the act expects adult adoptees not only to have access to their birth certificates, but that challenges will be made in order to view agency and court records.

The Commentaries are stronger than the act in supporting an adult adoptee's right to know. They declare,

> the original birth certificate will be opened to the adoptee who attained majority upon the adoptee's single request, no court order or intervention is required. Hence, the adult adoptee may by right obtain information identifying his birth parents. . . .

> Adoption, as a positive process designed to provide children with loving and stable homes, does not inherently require secrecy. . . . Foreign countries and states which allow adult adoptees access to their original birth certificates have not found that this access leads to widespread efforts at reunion with birth parents, or to disrupted adoptive families.

> [Moreover] the policy that adoption is a service to adoptees, and the preamble's guiding principle that when irreconcilable conflicts arise, the adoptee's rights should prevail, lead to the approach taken in this provision. Underlying the provision is a presumption that the adult adoptee is most capable of defining what is in his/her own welfare, including whether or not inspection of his/her original birth certificate would serve his interests. Unless the Model Act accorded all parties' interests equal stature and required courts to balance those interests on a case-by-case basis, the adoptee's right to information regarding his/her origins must prevail over the birth parents' presumed interest in anonymity.

> In summary, a number of considerations support the right of adult adoptees to view the original records of their birth: the increasing emphasis given to an individual's right to know and maintain his heritage, and principles of social work practice, including that of self-determination—the right of a person to determine his destiny according to his potential for growth and change. Alternative approaches to the problem of access to adoption records, such as the creation of a registry in which consents to information or contact could be filled by birth parents and adoptees, or the requirement that good cause be shown before access is granted, are favored by many, but are less in keeping with philosophy and purposes of the Model Act.[18]

Right to Know and Transracial Adoption

As the Commentaries demonstrate, the concept of an adult adoptee's right to know is gaining endorsement and acceptance. The desire to examine one's birth records would appear to us to be even stronger for transracially adopted than for inracially adopted adults. Transracial adoptees normally realize by themselves that they have not been born into their family. Thus a transracial adoptee would not only have the same natural curiosity as any other adopted individual, but his or her different background would probably intensify the already strong natural desire to know. The case would be particularly strong if the adoptee is black, as are so many in our study. The slogans of the 1960s (for example, "black is beautiful") have probably enhanced racial awareness on the part of all racial-ethnic minorities but especially among young blacks. Because black transracial adoptees live in a racially polarized society, they carry a double burden. They must not only reconcile who they are as adoptees, but also must come to terms with which world to fit into as a black transracial adoptee. The satisfactory solution of these questions is crucial to individual fulfillment.

In relating the issue of sealed records to transracial adoption, it is important to note research findings among parents who adopted inracially. Pannor surveyed 60 adoptive parents. His focus was, "Parents' attitudes toward their children's birth parents and their feelings about the adequacy of the background information provided to them at the time of the adoption." According to Pannor, as reported in Soronsky, Baran, and Pannor,

> Most of the adoptive parents indicated that they had an understanding, accepting, and sympathetic attitude toward the birth mother. In marked contrast to this, only a small number had positive feelings toward the birth father, with an overwhelming number expressing varying degrees of negative or indifferent feelings.
>
> Twenty-five percent were pleased with the amount of information they had received on the birth mother: 50 percent desired more information; and the remaining 50 percent had mixed reactions, including the feeling that giving too much information could actually be a burden to them.[19]

Soronsky also reports that as their work around the sealed-records issue gained more publicity, they received many letters from adoptive parents expressing their views about the issue. Soronsky divided the responses into five categories:

> The first group expressed an awareness of their adopted children's needs and a willingness to assist them in any way possible, including helping them search for their birth parents at adulthood.
>
> The second group wanted their children to have the right to seek their birth parents when they reached adulthood, but were adamant that the right to seek their relinquished child should not extend to birth parents.
>
> The third group could not see any reason for the study because they view their adopted children as happy, uninterested in their backgrounds, and totally committed to their adoptive family.

The fourth group expressed hostility toward the study and resented any en-croachment upon the sanctity of the sealed record agreement.

A fifth group focused upon their concern for the birth parents who had been promised anonymity.[20]

About the adoptees' reactions, Soronsky comments:

Our research data and case histories of adoptees corroborated our initial impression that adoptees are more vulnerable than non-adoptees to identity conflicts in late adolescence and young adulthood. Many of these adoptees seem preoccupied with existential concerns and have feelings of isolation and alienation resulting from the breaks in the continuity of life through the generations that their adoption represents. For some, the existing block to the past may create a feeling that there is a block to the future as well. The adoptee's identity formation must be viewed within the context of the life cycle, in which birth and death are linked unconsciously. This is evident in the frequency with which marriage, the birth of a child, or the death of adoptive parents triggers an even greater sense of interest in the birth parents.

It would appear that very few adoptees are provided with enough background information to incorporate into their developing ego and sense of identity. The adoptive parents are reluctant to impart known informa-tion, especially any of a negative nature, that might hurt the child. The adoptees in turn are often reluctant to ask genealogical questions because they sense their parents' insecurities in these areas. Information given to adoptive couples at the time of adoption is scanty and usually describes im-mature, confused, adolescent unwed mothers and fathers.

We believe that all adoptees have a desire to know about their origins. However, those adoptees who are basically curious and questioning in-dividuals appear, from our study, to be more likely to initiate a search and reunion. This is not necessarily related to the quality of the adoptive family relationship, although some adoptees' searches are based upon neurotic needs or poor nurturing.

What stands out most in our study of reunion cases are the positive benefits the majority of the adoptees gained. More important was the effect upon the adoptee who was able to resolve the conflicts of his/her dual identity.

It is our conviction that adult adoptees should have access to their birth records if they so desire, when they reach the age of eighteen. For those adoptees who are determined to find their birth parents, the information available in the original birth records may not be sufficient. In order to avoid situations where adoptees spend agonizing years and large sums of money tracking down trivial clues, we would support methods to facilitate the search. Regional or national registries where adoptees and birth parents could indicate their interest in reunion, for example, have been suggested. In addition, agencies could provide identifying information and reunion services upon request.[21]

In conclusion, the author recommended the following:

1. The opening of original birth records to adult adoptees and the providing of background and identifying information to them on request.
2. The establishment of appropriate boards available to intercede, on a voluntary basis, on behalf of those adult adoptees and birth parents who wish to affect a reunion.
3. Continuing commitments by adoption agencies to all members of the adoption triangle for as long as necessary, including the provision of viable, current information to any of these parties. This will require the re-establishment and continuation of contact by the agency with the adoptive family and birth parents.
4. The establishment of counseling services which recognize that adoption is a lifelong process for all involved.
5. Consideration on the part of the authorities of new adoption alternatives to provide stable homes and families for children who would not be relinquished otherwise.[22]

Because of the intense interest around the issue of open records in the past few years and because of its special relevance for our respondents, we included a question about it in our follow-up survey. We asked:

In the last few years there has been quite a lot of discussion about "open records." Has your adopted child(ren) asked you directly or tried to find out in any other way about his or her biological parents and family?

About 60 percent of our adoptive parents (mothers and fathers) reported that their adopted children expressed at least mild interest in the topic.

Most of the parents perceived their child's interest and curiosity matter of factly and did not draw any conclusions from it. One mother characterized her reactions as follows:

I have shared all the information I have about R's, J's, and T's parents, including their mothers' names, which I requested from our lawyer. We asked the kids if they wanted to know the names and they did. They are fascinated with names and details surrounding their birth and details about their birth parents. No one has asked if he could try to meet his biological parent yet, but I wouldn't be surprised if someday they might think it is important to meet them. I will help them if they want to try to solve that aspect of their identity by meeting their birth parents. I can see how an adopted son could be curious and feel somehow cut off from part of himself or herself.

Table A-1
Children's Interest in Biological Parents, by Sex of Responding Parent

Parent	Report that Children Expressed		
	No Interest	Mild Interest	Strong Interest
Mother	40%	42%	18%
Father	39	44	17

This response is typical for children who have expressed interest. A few parents, particularly in families experiencing problems with an adopted child, interpreted the child's interest as a feeling of insecurity or as a test for the adopted parents. One family had adopted an Indian boy who had been in three foster homes by the time he was adopted when he was seven months old. (At the time of the survey he was twelve.) In explaining a problem with their son, the father wrote:

> We have been very candid with all we know about V's biological mother and background. He is very interested in this information, but seems to be satisfied with our explanations and with his present family situation. However, I feel he still is testing our willingness to keep him, even after eleven years of adoption.[23]

We received the following response from the mother in another family that was having difficulties with their black adopted daughter. (At eight years old she was having racial-identity problems.) The mother wrote,

> E [their other ten-year-old black adopted daughter] asks occasionally about her mother in particular, and we are prepared to help her find her parents at a later date. Y [the child with whom they are having problems] is too insecure to discuss it yet. Since we are her 5th family, I think she doesn't want to press her luck by inquiring about anyone in the past that she might be sent back to.

Another mother said that she did not know how to enhance her black daughter's self-image (the daughter is nine years old) and that she felt frustrated and confused. She answered the question this way:

> Yes, she has expressed some interest. She seems confused about her "other" mother. We have explained adoption in terms of love and personal selection, but I, too, feel the need for L to seek out her biological parents eventually.

In studying all the responses to our query, we could find no pattern that correlated the children's interest or lack of interest with their sex, race, or ordinal position in the family. As noted in the preceding paragraphs, some parents did relate time spent in foster homes with their children's interest or lack of interest in finding out where they came from.

While our question specifically concerned the adoptees' interests, we also received reactions and comments from two thirds of the parents about their own attitudes and beliefs on the issue. We think they are worth sharing. First of all, the reactions ran eight to one in favor of the adopted children's right to know and need to find their biological parents, especially their mothers. Both the adoptive mothers and fathers shared this belief. Almost all of them said that they would help their children locate information about their biological parents after they were eighteen or twenty-one years old.

One of the parents captured the sentiments of many when he said,

> I am not threatened by this as it is no reflection on our love, rather just an innate need to know.
>
> T is interested in meeting his biological parents and possibly his other family. He wants to know if I want to meet them. I want him to be able to pursue this without fear that I would be hurt or unhappy. I would be nervous, but I feel he has this right.

For children adopted from Vietnam, the likelihood of tracing their parents seems remote. One adoptee's mother described what she learned:

> Both daughters wish they could at least see a picture of their birth mother. There isn't that much interest in their father. Records in Vietnam are practically non-existent, so tracking their background/parent is probably unrealistic. I tried to find out as much as possible from the orphanage. However, most of us were told the same story: the child was born in a hospital, and when the mother disappeared, the child was taken to an orphanage.

The father wrote,

> The contact we did have with the orphanage at the time of the children's adoption has largely dissolved with the new regime.

One of the mothers, who is herself an adopted child, wrote,

> As a matter of fact, I went through a search myself trying to find my biological mother. I have been working with "Yesterday's Children." R [her daughter] knew about this, and I told her that if ever she wanted to search for her parents, I would help her in whatever ways I could. She said at the time she had no need to do this. "Why tamper with what I have?" She may, of course, change her mind as she gets older. She has wondered why she was given away, but satisfied in believing that her parents were too young and irresponsible for parenthood to keep her.

Three of the families have located their adopted children's birth records. One of these adoptive mothers explained,

> I worked as a volunteer at the adoption agency that gave us our son. I got the biological parents' name for him [her son]. He has not yet met his biological parents.

Another of these families has given their adopted son a copy of his birth record that contains the name of his biological parents. "We've told him this is his special information to share with us if he wishes. And that it is not ours to share, except with him."

About one in eight parents expressed negative views or fears about their children's interest and desire to know more about their biological parents. Their reactions betray feelings that if the children have a need to search out their biological parents, they have failed in some way as parents or have not met all the emotional needs of their adopted children. They are explicit about feeling threatened by their children's inquiries and by their desires to locate their birth parents.

Other responses demonstrated concern for protecting the biological parents as well as the children. In one family the father wrote,

> I personally oppose open records. Persons may have excellent reasons for records to remain closed. I would hope Wisconsin would not follow Illinois' dubious lead in this area.

And the mother said, "I believe open records could be damaging to child, parent, biological parent, and their new life."

The most unusual response to this question came from a mother of five children, four of whom had been adopted and two of whom are transracially adopted. The mother wrote that one of her white adopted children wanted to be returned to his birth parents. She was having difficulties relating to him at that period, and she claimed that she considered placing ads in various media to try and locate the boy's biological parents. The mother commented, "The social worker and psychologist had fits," when they heard of her plan. She has not yet carried through on it.

Parents who adopt transracially do not have the same option available to more traditional adopters. They cannot ignore the children's status in the family and thereby allow the adopted children to assume that they were born into the family. Perhaps because all the parents in our survey have had to acknowledge to the children that they were adopted, the great majority do not find their children's interests and curiosity about their birth parents as painful or traumatic as the authors of the *Adoption Triangle* suggest. Most of them reported that they have offered to help their children trace their records in the hope that they might be able to locate either the parents (especially the mother) or some information about them. Most were not threatened by the prospect of having their adopted children learn about or have contacts with their biological families. The children are not yet old enough to test their parents' verbal commitment. We will have to wait until they are adults to judge the strength of their parents' resolve.

Notes

1. Carolyn Burke, "The Adult Adoptee's Constitutional Right to Know His Origins," *Southern California Law Review* 48 (May 1975):1196-

1220; C.L. Gaylord, "The Adoptive Child's Right to Know," *Case and Comment* 81 (March-April 1976):38-44; Arthur D. Soronsky, Annette Baran, and Reuben Pannor, *The Adoptive Triangle* (Anchor Press, New York, 1978); Barbara Prager and Stanley Rothstein, "The Adoptee's Right to Know His Natural Heritage," *New York Law Forum* 19 (Summer 1973):137-156.

2. Prager and Rothstein, "The Adoptee's Right to Know."

3. Susan Heller Anderson, "The Adoptee's Right to Know: Study Calls British Law a Success," *New York Times*, 18 March 1980, p. C-12.

4. *U.S. Statutes at Large* 92 (1978):2069.

5. House Report 95-1386 (1978), *U.S. Code Congressional and Administrative News*, 1978, p. 7725.

6. Anderson, "The Adoptee's Right to Know."

7. Joseph D. Harrington, "Legislative Reform Moves Slowly," *Public Welfare* 37 (No. 3) (Summer 1979):57. This article also contains an excellent review of current legislation regarding open records.

It should also be noted that a lesser known group favors retaining sealed-record statutes. The Association for the Protection of the Adoptive Triangle, a nationwide group of adoptive parents, seeks to prevent repeal of sealed-records laws. The chances are that this organization is in a much weaker position to have its goals met than are the previously mentioned groups favoring repeal.

8. Soronsky, Baran, and Pannor, *The Adoptive Triangle*, p. 25.

9. Ibid., p. 26.

10. Michael Shapiro, *A Study of Adoption Practice*, Vol. 1 (Child Welfare League of America, New York, 1956), p. 14; Gaylord, "The Adoptive Child's Right to Know"; and Kenneth Watson, "Who Is the Primary Client?" *Public Welfare* 37 (No. 3) (Summer 1971):11.

11. Kenneth Watson, "Who Is the Primary Client?" *Child Welfare* 37 (No. 3) (Summer 1971):11.

12. Gaylord, "The Adoptive Child's Right to Know" (Ref.: *Lawson* v. *Registrar-General*, 1956, 106, L.J. 204.

It is interesting to note here that since England enacted the Children's Act in 1975, allowing adult adoptees access to their birth records, only 1 to 2 percent of all adult adoptees have requested the information. (Anderson, "The Adoptee's Right to Know").

13. Burke, "The Adult Adoptee's Constitutional Right." Reprinted with permission.

14. *NASW News* 25 (No. 1) (Washington, D.C.: NASW, January 1980):20.

15. Child Welfare League of America, *Standards for Adoption Service*, revised, section 4.27 (1978), pp. 54-55.

16. Child Welfare League of America, *Standards for Adoption Service* (Child Welfare League of America, New York, 1973).

17. Model State Adoption Act and Commentaries, Title V, "Records," *Federal Register*, (Feb. 1980), sections 501 and 502, pp. 10638-10639.

18. Ibid., subsection D, p. 10687.

19. Soronsky, Baran, and Pannor, *The Adoptive Triangle*, pp. 68-69. Copyright © 1978 by Arthur D. Soronsky, Annette Baran, and Reuben Pannor. Reprinted by permission of Doubleday & Company, Inc.

20. Ibid., pp. 70-73.

21. Ibid., pp. 229-231.

22. Ibid., pp. 232-233.

23. The boy had stolen things from his older sister and does not get along with his brother.

Appendix B
Model State Adoption
Act and Model State
Adoption Procedures

This appendix was prepared for two reasons: (1) to present the most current (1981) judicial thinking regarding adoption; and (2) to indicate grudging acceptance of transracial adoption by legislators and policymakers.

Lawmakers are reluctant to endorse transracial adoption publicly, although the Model State Adoption Act alludes to it in several instances. It is reasonable to assume that there is a connection between the shyness of adoption policymakers and the power of transracial-adoption opponents.

The Department of Health and Human Services published the Model State Adoption Act and Model State Adoption Procedures (the act) in the *Federal Register* in 1980.[1] It includes a commentary prepared by the Model Adoption Legislation and Procedures Advisory Panel in conjunction with the American Public Welfare Association. The act stems from the Child Abuse Prevention and Treatment and Adoption Reform Act of 1978, discussed in chapter 3.[2] In the entire 77-page document, transracial adoption is referred to only obliquely and never discussed operationally. This omission is curious in light of the attention the issue has received in the last 10 years.

This appendix discusses and interprets those sections of the act and commentary that have implications for transracial adoption. It is important to note that the act is comprehensive, dealing with the full scope of adoption. It is not a statute. It will be forwarded to the states for their consideration. As its title indicates, it is to serve as a model for their use. Individual states may accept it in its entirety, accept only some of its provisions, or reject it totally.

Inracial and Transracial Adoption

The preamble to the act states,

> The legislation affirms the importance of family life for all children. The state declares adoption a positive social and legal process to make family life possible for children whose parents cannot or choose not to rear them. The law's express commitment to serve all children who are older, who are minority race. . . . The Act acknowledges the need for adoption to reflect the adoptee's racial . . . heritage, but indicates that these considerations should *not* [authors' emphasis] be a barrier to adoption. This philosophy must be reflected in agency policies in recruitment of families and in placement practices.[3]

The act appears not only to endorse the concept of transracial adoption ["these (racial) considerations should not be a barrier to adoption."] but states that the placement of children across racial lines must be considered by agencies in recruiting potential adoptive parents and in the agencies' placement practices. As with most official documents, the act does not define transracial adoption specifically. Transracial adoption is seen as an operating concept consistent with society's attempts to reduce racial barriers.

The commentary reinforces the favorable disposition toward transracial adoption implied in the preamble:

> To increase the likelihood that children who need adoption services are identified and then placed for adoption, the Model Act focuses on ameliorating or eliminating various obstacles to adoption existing in present law and practice. Negative attitudes about adopted children, restrictive eligibility criteria established by agencies for adoptive parents. . . .[4]

> Placements for adoption and other plans for children made pursuant to the Act should, whenever possible, reasonably protect each child's heritage. While differences in race, religion, or ethnicity will not be a bar to adoption, every effort should be made to place a child with a family of like heritage. In the event that such a family cannot be found, and a transcultural [for example, transracial adoption, authors' addition] placement is made, the implication of such an adoption must be made clear to all parties involved.[5]

Thus the commentary adds concrete direction to the preamble's indirect reference to transracial adoption. It states that transcultural placement (transracial adoption) is a distinct plan of action even though "every effort should be made to place a child with a family of like heritage."

To the best of our knowledge, this has been the practice in most transracial placements. We know of no case in which there has been any large-scale, conscious attempt to deny an available child to an adoptive family of the same race. This does not deny isolated, discretionary actions by individual child-care workers. These must be considered subjective. All honest social workers know of cases in which favorite foster families were given a certain type of child or allowed to maintain a child longer than necessary because that placement was considered to be better for the child than a more permanent setting.

The commentary states,

> The implications of such an adoption [transracial, authors' addition] must be made clear to all parties involved.

Several recent studies deal with the effects of transracial adoption on "all parties involved."[6]

The act also refers to transracial adoption (in all but name) in Title II, Placement for Adoption,[7] and in the commentary to the act.[8] Section 205 states,

> Applicants for children designated as waiting for adoption because of age, race, color, . . . must be given priority for a family assessment by the agency. . . .
>
> Since the goal is to provide the child with a stable, nurturing home and since the field of social work acknowledges the validity of a variety of parenting styles, agencies cannot restrict the eligibility of applicants solely on the basis of such factors as age, race. . . .
>
> Because of the need for flexibility in determining which families meet the needs of individual children, all applicants deserve consideration. Rigid arbitrary eligibility criteria eliminate opportunities for children to benefit from the experience of family life. Therefore, the maintenance of such restrictive criteria by an agency cannot be justified.

The act establishes the principle that if adoptive parents of the same race cannot be located for an available child, transracial adoption should be considered. In fact, the prospective (transracially) adoptive parent "must be given priority for a family assessment by the agency."[9]

The act favors one of the basic premises of transracial adoption: that preconceived or arbitrary racial limitations to child placement are undemocratic and that a permanent, loving family environment of whatever variant is in the child's best interest and in the interest of all concerned [for example, adoptive parents and siblings, society, and biological parent(s)].

The act states that "the field of social work acknowledges the validity of a variety of parenting styles. . . ." This reflects the current official position in the social-work profession as well as increasing recognition by the courts that child rearing can no longer be limited to the traditional nuclear family, composed of a set of parents and biological offspring of the same race (see chapter 2).

Recruitment

Recruitment, or the lack of it, is consistently linked to the rise of transracial adoption. The act specifically discusses recruitment in several sections but never directly links the dearth of nonwhite adopters to the disproportionate availability of nonwhite children:

> Aggressive recruitment programs must be designed by the agency to attract families for children awaiting adoption.[10]
>
> Recruitment of adoptive homes for children waiting because of age, race, handicap . . . is a service to children that brings results.

Recruitment programs must be adequately funded and staffed in order to include contacts with mass media, local community organizations, and adoptive parents' organizations, as well as with groups with a special interest in certain types of children, such as those with cerebral palsy or mental retardation.[11]

Strategies to assist recruitment of parents include "flyers for inclusion in bank mailings . . . , distribution with consumer goods, brochures, posters, bumper stickers, television and radio public service announcements . . . "). The issue of nonwhite recruitment is not specifically addressed even though nonwhite children constitute one of the largest groups of all the hard-to-place children available for adoption. If sufficient numbers of nonwhite adopters were recruited for available nonwhite children, the controversy surrounding transracial adoption could be put to rest. Still, no mention is made of this.

Rather, this section singles out groups such as children with cerebral palsy or mental retardation. While these children certainly warrant special attention, their number is considerably smaller than the number of nonwhite adoptable children. As we have noted, the basic argument of individuals and groups against transracial adoption is that it would be unnecessary if agencies aggressively sought potential nonwhite adopters.

Recruitment of potential nonwhite adopters is only referred to in the act in a broad context. For example, it is mentioned under "Public Information Programs":

This information [regarding adoption programs and services] should be prepared with consideration given to the needs of different racial and ethnic groups and the need for publications in different languages;[12]

and under, "Training Programs":

Areas to be covered in the training programs might include, but should not be limited to . . . recruiting families [including minority families]. . . .[13]

The act implies that recruitment of potential nonwhite adopters, although important and necessary, is not a *critical* problem worthy of special consideration.

The commentary attached to the act is more direct regarding the recruitment of nonwhite adopters, but it also places the issue within a larger category. The commentary declares,

The identification of children in need of adoption, removal of obstacles to their adoption, and vigorous recruitment of appropriate adoptive families are all express purposes of the Act. . . .[14]

One can assume that "vigorous recruitment of appropriate adoptive families" was intended to include an active search for nonwhite adopters for nonwhite children. The commentary goes on to say,

> Closely related to the state's duty to oversee active recruitment of adoptive parents suitable to the population of waiting children is the duty to provide family assessments to applicants who respond to these special recruitment efforts. . . . The value of providing these assessments to all persons who express an interest in adopting a "hard-to-place" child cannot be overemphasized.[15] Public information and education is an essential part of the recruitment process.

The most innovative and creative recruitment programs will not be totally successful unless the accompanying process and methods of selecting potential adoptive parents are likewise innovative and creative. Too many prospective parents have been screened out of the adoption process because they do not match traditional established criteria. As a result, only a few blue-ribbon families are selected for similar children.

Recruitment and Subsidies

The last section of the act examines financial subsidies for potential adopters—the most successful recruitment device thus far.[16] The act quickly and rather superficially links the two ideas of recruitment and subsidies:

> Aggressive recruitment programs must be designed by the agency to attract families for children awaiting adoption. . . . An agency may expect a considerable number of inquiries following any specialized recruitment activity. . . .
>
> The agency should inform applicants of the approximate time the assessment will take, eligibility standards, types of children available for placement, availability of subsidy. . . .[17]

Subsidized adoption is examined as part of an overall recruitment program in Title VII of the act. Section 701 implies that subsidies should aid in attracting potential adopters to hard-to-place children.

> The purpose of a subsidy is to assure the most appropriate adoption through public financial subsidy for each child who might not otherwise be adopted. The children who might not otherwise be adopted are those with physical, emotional, or mental handicaps, minority children, older children, and family groups. . . . The subsidy program serves as a supplement to an effective recruitment program for adoptive families and provides an additional resource for the children who are waiting.[18]

The inclusion of "minority children" among "children who might not otherwise be adopted" brings in the issue of transracial adoption.

Section 702, "Administration," discusses subsidies and recruitment further:

> The availability of subsidies for children must be publicized in every possible way:
>
> Agencies must inform all foster and adoptive parents about the program.
>
> Descriptions of subsidies should be included in all written materials about adoption, especially recruitment materials.
>
> Public information meetings should include a segment dealing with subsidies.[19]

Sections 701 and 702 acknowledge the value of publicizing subsidies to encourage potential adopters. While the proponents of subsidies do not believe that a family would adopt a child only in order to obtain the subsidy, the availability of a subsidy may be the single most important factor in determining the family's decision to adopt.

Section 703, "Eligibility for Subsidy," describes the conditions under which a child could receive a subsidy. It is not a test to establish the eligibility of a prospective adoptive family for a subsidy. They are provided directly for the care of hard-to-place children. They are not intended to serve as economic incentives to potential adopters who are financially unable to adopt at all. Subsidies are available for specific children whose specific conditions prevent them from being adopted.

> The child's social worker prepares the necessary documents for the child's certificate for subsidy. . . .
>
> Special documentation pertaining to the child's particular handicap or other condition of eligibility . . . such things as the child's need for special schooling or tutoring, prostheses, and special clothing, as well as the diagnosis, prognosis, and future plans for treatment of the condition.[20]

It is interesting to note that during the Senate's debate of HR3434, an amendment was proposed to remove federal assistance from adoption programs:

> While . . . there is a need to find good and stable homes for parentless children . . . [adoption] demands a deeper commitment and a permanent relationship with a child and stems from the fact there is only one right reason to adopt . . . because the child is loved and wanted as one's own.[21]

No matter how much a couple wanted to adopt a child, only the rich would be able to adopt a child who required expensive care or medical treatment. Most adopters are middle class.

Where other than physical conditions reduce children's chances of being adopted, the act suggests a somewhat different approach:

> For other factors such as age, race, ethnicity, or the need to be placed with siblings, documentation should include a record of referral to state, regional, and national exchanges, or referral to a specialized adoption agency. The documentation should show that the referrals did not result in the location of a family for the child within 60 days after they were made.[22]

"State, regional, and national exchanges" use various procedures: biographies, pictures, and so on of children available for adoption are circulated to various adoption agencies or in some cases to television and radio media outside of the child's area to attract potential adopters. The stipulation of adoption exchange referral is included to demonstrate that "reasonable efforts have been made to place the child without subsidy."[23]

According to Title VII of the commentary, widespread use of adoption subsidies began in New York in 1968.[24] Its popularity is based on economics. Individual states support subsidized adoption because it is the least costly method of family child care. Adoption-subsidy funds are drawn from foster-care funds in most states, although some states make specific allocations for subsidized adoption. Connecting adoption subsidies to foster-care allowances has the added advantage of tying adoption to the least expensive child-care program. For example, in 1980 Massachusetts paid $7-12,000 per child year for foster care, $11-19,000 for group home living, and $30-60,000 for institutionalization.[25]

The commentary reinforces the act's two main premises regarding subsidies, linking them to both recruitment programs for prospective adopters and to the child.

> It [subsidized adoption] is not intended to discourage vigorous recruitment of the most desirable adoptive families. . . . However, when no adoptive family can be found for a child, it is appropriate to consider providing *that child* [authors' emphasis] with an adoption subsidy.[26]

From the act, it would appear that transracial adoption is an idea whose time is yet to come officially. While it is all but implied in some of the act's titles, nowhere is it directly endorsed, supported, or suggested as a means of alleviating the chronic impermanence of this major group of parentless children.

Even its most ardent supporters do not view transracial adoption as a panacea for our child-welfare ills. To the concept entirely, however, is an injustice to those parentless children for whom it would be an appropriate placement.

Notes

1. Model State Adoption Act and Commentaries, Part V. The *Federal Register* (15 Feb. 1980) is intended to serve both as a report to the public and as a request for comments.
2. In particular, Title II, section 203 of (PL 95-266) the Child Abuse Prevention and Treatment and Adoption Reform Act, passed in April 1978.
3. Model State Adoption Act, p. 10624.
4. Ibid., p. 10648.
5. Ibid., p. 10650.
6. See Rita Simon and Howard Altstein, *Transracial Adoption* (Wiley Interscience, New York, 1977); Lucille J. Grow and Deborah Shapiro, *Black Children—White Parents: A Study of Transracial Adoption* (Child Welfare League of America, New York, 1974), p. 88; Dawn Day, *The Adoption of Black Children* (Lexington, Mass.: Lexington Books, D.C. Heath and Company, 1979); and Joyce A. Ladner, *Mixed Families* (Anchor/Doubleday, Garden City, New York, 1977).
7. Model State Adoption Act, section 205, "Placement for Adoption by Agencies," (a) Priority of Family Assessments and (b) Eligibility of Applicants, p. 10628.
8. Ibid., p. 10661.
9. Ibid., p. 10628.
10. Ibid., section 205.
11. Ibid., section 601, p. 10641.
12. Ibid., subsection 9(e), "Public Information Programs," p. 10642.
13. Ibid., section 601, "Training Programs," p. 10643.
14. Ibid., p. 10651.
15. Ibid., p. 10693.
16. See Simon and Altstein, *Transracial Adoption*, chapter 7, for a brief historical overview.
17. Model State Adoption Act, p. 10629.
18. Ibid., section 701, p. 10646.
19. Ibid., section 702, "Administration," p. 10646.
20. Ibid., section 703, "Eligibility for Subsidy," p. 10646.
21. American Public Welfare Association, W-Menw #38, Washington, D.C., 6 November 1979.
22. Model State Adoption Act, p. 10646.

23. Ibid.

24. For a detailed examination of subsidized adoption, see Simon and Altstein, *Transracial Adoption*, chapter 7.

25. *NASW News* 25 (No. 3) (March 1980):4.

26. Model State Adoption Act, p. 10692.

Appendix C
Guidelines for
Transracial Adoption
Participants

The Interracial Family Association supports the interracial family as a viable life style, and transracial adoption as a viable means of achieving that life style. This paper translates that support of transracial adoption into specific guidelines which we believe should be recognized by prospective transracial adoptive families, and utilized by placement agencies or groups.

We support and encourage the placement of all children in permanent homes with parents who love, cherish and nurture them. We value the ethnic heritage of our interracial children and are concerned that parents being considered for such children are aware of the commitment they are making to provide that child with a racial identity.

1. We believe that participants in transracial placements should be aware there is opposition to such placements, not only from the historic prejudice to interracial marriage. . . . peoples, Black social workers, and many other ethnic groups struggling for political and cultural identity. Many social workers prefer a matched placement—and matched means physical and cultural similarities of child to adoptive parents.
2. We feel the prospective family should have broad acceptance of other racial backgrounds than their own. It is not enough for a parent to want a child and accept this other race child as a last resort.
3. We believe prospective adoptive parents should value, respect and be supportive of their children's heritages. What have they done to learn more about this heritage so that they can provide the child a cultural orientation?
4. We feel individual support may not be enough to sustain a child within the family. Association with an interracial group, whether a church, a synagogue, a community, a parent group, a business or a significant number of friends and associates of this child's racial background, may provide additional social support and acceptance.
5. We believe parents of an interracial or minority child should be flexible enough to consider a change in life style or attitudes as a result of this adoptive placement. We feel interracial parents must be aware of the extent and forms of racism in their own environment against members of this race.
6. We feel experienced transracial families should be utilized by agencies as a resource in pre- and post-adoptive counseling.

With these criteria in mind, we can support transracial adoption and know that the future of minority children is not being jeopardized by placement of children with parents unaware of what race means in America.

"Transracial Adoption Position Paper," Part II, Interracial Family Association Board, Seattle, Washington, adopted 13 December 1977.

Index

About the Authors

Rita J. Simon is professor of sociology, law, and communications at the University of Illinois, Urbana. Her published works include, among others, *Transracial Adoption*, *The Jury: Its Role in American Society* (Lexington Books, 1980), *Women and Crime* (Lexington Books, 1975), *Continuity and Change: A Study of Two Ethnic Communities in Israel*, and *The Jury and the Defense of Insanity*. Professor Simon served as editor of the American Sociological Review from 1978-1980. She has been a visiting professor at Hebrew University in Jerusalem.

Howard Altstein is an associate professor and chairman of the research sequence in the School of Social Work and Community Planning at the University of Maryland. He was formerly director of the school's research center. In fall 1981 he will assume the directorship of the school's doctoral program. He has written primarily in the area of child welfare, particularly on foster care and adoption. He is especially interested in examining the connection between research findings and child-welfare practice.